Overcoming Common Problems Series

Overcoming Common Problems Series

Overcoming Common Problems

COPING SUCCESSFULLY WITH AGORAPHOBIA

Dr Kenneth Hambly

SHELDON PRESS
LONDON

First published in Great Britain in 1992
Sheldon Press, SPCK, Marylebone Road, London NW1 4DU

© Dr Kenneth Hambly 1992

British Library Cataloguing-in-Publication Data
A catalogue record for this book is available from the British Library
ISBN 0–85969–648–0

Photoset by Deltatype Ltd, Ellesmere Port, Cheshire
Printed in Great Britain by Courier International Ltd, East Kilbride

Contents

Preface

The term 'agoraphobia' comes from two Greek words meaning (roughly), 'fear of open spaces'. Nowadays that means fear of supermarkets, busy streets, railway stations or almost anywhere where there are other people. It is a condition from which many people suffer, and those who suffer from it find it a mystifying and often disturbing problem which limits their lives and can bring them to the point of despair. It appears to be completely illogical; it defies understanding – or so it seems.

Things are not always what they seem, however. Agoraphobia *is* a logical condition once you understand it, and it can be overcome if you go about it the right way. It takes some hard work, of course, but if you make the effort you can overcome agoraphobia and lead a completely normal life. It isn't easy, but if you suffer from agoraphobia the rewards for your efforts will be immense.

If you find going out in public difficult, if you are uncomfortable in a supermarket or just walking down the street, you may find it impossible to believe that you will be able to lead a normal life untroubled by feelings of fear, and yet it is possible to do just that. This book will unravel the mysteries of agoraphobia and explain how it is caused, how it works, what keeps it going, and, much more important, how you can go about overcoming your problem.

No matter how severe your agoraphobia may be, or how long you have suffered from it, or how desperate you may feel, there is a solution to your problem. The first step to overcoming your agoraphobia is to read this book. It gives straightforward, common-sense advice on how to deal with your problem, and that is all you need to get started on your road to a new life.

Let's give it a try!

1

What is Agoraphobia?

Imagine that you are standing in the middle of a supermarket. It is busy, and there are queues at all of the checkouts. People are rushing to finish their shopping, pushing and jostling. You are by yourself. Now you have to stand in a long queue with people patiently waiting for their turn at the checkout. You can't leave your shopping trolley, there is no other way out, you have to stay in the queue. Really try to imagine that you are in that situation, standing there, trapped in that queue. How do you feel? What is your body doing to you right now?

If you are now feeling uncomfortable, if you are feeling sweaty, if your heart is racing and if your muscles are tight, then you know what agoraphobia is. Your imagination is a potent instrument, and for some people even thinking about a threatening situation can bring on those awful feelings and they will experience that rising panic. It can be worse than that. You may wake up in the morning feeling uncomfortable and apprehensive before you remember why, almost as if your body knows that you have to go to the supermarket this day before your mind realizes it.

Even if you don't experience those unpleasant feelings when you think about difficult situations, if you suffer from agoraphobia you will recognize them because you will experience them when you are in the supermarket, or the bank, or even just walking down the street. You may have been avoiding these things for years, or you may have been able to do them only with the greatest difficulty. You may have been embarrassed by your problem and kept it a secret, but your problem has not gone away, and it may have been getting worse. Let's consider a typical case of someone who suffers from agoraphobia.

I am a general practitioner with an interest in psychological problems, so many people come to discuss their difficulties with me. Joanne was one such person, a young married woman in her early thirties with two children, a boy and a girl. It had taken her some time to pluck up the courage to come and see me, but when she did she was able to talk about her problems with just a little encouragement. She came with her husband, Jimmy, and this is what she had to say:

Joanne

I never was a nervous person, but about three years ago I began to feel nervous and edgy from time to time. It was worse when I was outside, and I would begin to feel uncomfortable as soon as I started to get ready to go out. When I was taking the children to playschool I would be shaky and tearful, and I used to dread meeting people. One day in the supermarket I had an attack of dizziness, and just had to leave the trolly and go out. It was very frightening. After that I couldn't face shopping by myself, and had to go with Jimmy. Even so it was an ordeal and eventually I stopped going altogether. I would feel ill even at the thought of going out, and couldn't contemplate doing it by myself. I've had to depend more and more on Jimmy. Now my life is hardly worth living. I live in fear of having to go out somewhere, anywhere. Just going out is a nightmare, and there seems to be no pleasure in life any more.

Joanne had reached the end of her tether, and was almost housebound. She was confused and frightened by the condition, and was so embarrassed by it that she had delayed seeking help as long as possible. By so doing she had missed out on part of her life. Agoraphobia is a common problem, and she should not have been embarrassed to admit that she suffered from it. With even the most basic of advice, the problem became less troublesome. Indeed, the very act of talking about it seemed to make it easier.

Your agoraphobia is probably nothing like as bad as Joanne's, but it might still disrupt your life to a great extent, and you may well have to organize your day-to-day living carefully so as to avoid those situations which make you feel so uncomfortable. As a result your life may be less happy and less fulfilled than it should be, and you deserve better than that.

Why do you feel so bad in certain situations?

What actually happens when you go out into a public place if you suffer from agoraphobia? The simple answer is that you experience fear. But why should you be afraid of going into a public place? What could happen to you? You can be sure that the ground isn't going to open and swallow you up, so what are you afraid of?

The dictionary definition of a phobia is that it is an 'irrational fear', but that isn't good enough. You aren't an irrational person, so why would you have an irrational fear? Why should that fear be felt the morning of a threatening event? It doesn't make sense, and yet in the introduction to this book I talked about common sense and how it could help you to overcome your problem. It just doesn't add up – or does it?

You may have tried to work out just what it is that you are afraid of, and why you can't do the simple things that other people take for granted. What is wrong with you? Why do you feel this way? I was asked these questions by someone we will call David. He was troubled by agoraphobia, and he was distressed by just these problems.

David wondered why he was scared of going out into public places. He was a sports fan, but his enjoyment of sport was now reduced to watching it on television. He could no longer go into bars or public places. He felt panicky and unwell in open spaces, and it was worse in crowds. He was angry about the way he felt. I asked him to do an exercise for me. I asked him to tell me exactly what *symptoms* he experienced in his most threatening situation, and after some thought this is what he told me:

David

I feel a prickly feeling down my back, and I feel sweaty. My chest feels tight and I can't get a breath, so I breathe more

5

quickly. I feel shaky and my hand trembles. I can feel my heart thumping in my chest and my stomach churns as if I have diarrhoea. Sometimes I feel that I am going to be sick. Once I got suddenly very dizzy as if I was going to faint and had to hold on to a wall. That was a dreadful feeling which terrified me. I thought I was going to die. It happened at a football match and I haven't been back to one since.

Let's ask ourselves some questions. Were these symptoms which David described real, or were they just in his mind? Did he imagine them? What do you think? The answer is quite straightforward: every symptom which David described was entirely real, just as real as the pain of a broken leg. David suffered real distress in public places, and the symptoms he experienced were real and terrifying. So what was David scared of when he went into public places? The answer is that if he was scared at all he was scared of his very real, and very frightening, symptoms, and who wouldn't be? The symptoms which an agoraphobic person experiences in public places are real and they are very frightening, and only an idiot wouldn't be concerned about going into a situation which produces them.

There is therefore a distinction to be made between the fear which a person who suffers from agoraphobia certainly experiences, and the physical symptoms which produce that fear. You might think that it is the other way round, that it is fear which produces the symptoms, but that isn't the case. We can all experience fear in a dangerous situation, and that fear produces the same symptoms that an agoraphobic person experiences, but the agoraphobic person experiences these symptoms in quite inappropriate places, places which are not fearful, places in which he or she used to be comfortable and relaxed.

If you are agoraphobic your body produces symptoms in certain specific situations, and the production of those un-pleasant sensations, which are real and physical, is something over which you have no control. You don't appear to be able to do anything about it, so it's hardly surprising that you find it so disturbing.

Fear

If agoraphobia is just a collection of unpleasant physical symptoms experienced in specific locations, can we totally discount the idea of fear? Is there any fear associated with agoraphobia, and if so, is it just a fear that your symptoms will somehow do you some kind of harm? That may be part of it, and some people who suffer from agoraphobia say that when they have those feelings of panic they feel as if they are going to die, so it is no wonder that they feel fear. Deep down, however, most people realize that their symptoms will pass, and if they are in the safety of their own homes they will be fine. So what is this element of fear? That is something I discussed with another sufferer, a young man we will call Gareth.

Gareth always walked to work. As he walked along the main street, he would begin to tremble. His hand would shake, and he would feel dizzy and afraid. I asked him what *exactly* he was afraid of. I wanted him to tell me the precise thoughts which went through his head. This is what he told me:

Gareth

I feel unhappy as soon as I wake up, and that gets worse as I get up and have my breakfast. By the time I am ready to go out I am feeling terrified. When I start to walk I am frightened that my legs won't work property and that I may not be able to cross the road, or that I may fall. I think that someone will see me shaking and think that I am ill or worse, drunk. As I continue it feels as if I may break down and cry, and that I will make a public scene, and when I am really bad I worry that I may shout out and say something which will make me conspicuous, so that I make a fool of myself. It is a great relief to arrive at my work. The only problem is that I know that I will have to walk home again in the evening.

So just as there are many different symptoms which the agoraphobic sufferer can experience in difficult situations, there are many kinds of fear. But is that fear 'irrational', as the dictionary suggests it is? Well, if the symptoms are real, as I have suggested they are, then so are the fears. Gareth was worried about crossing roads, but then he had tension in the muscles in his legs and in his neck so that he felt stiff and awkward. Tense muscles produce a tremor so there is a reason for this and, indeed, for all of his symptoms, so was his fear about his difficulties real or imagined? Surely they were entirely rational fears of very real symptoms, and that is true for all of the fears he had. We will discuss them in detail later.

Agoraphobia as a physical condition

If agoraphobia were a physical condition like diabetes or asthma, people would not be so secretive about it. People are seldom secretive about physical conditions, but they certainly are about something which seems to be psychological or perhaps 'mental'. It's almost as if people think that they have some choice about their illness, that they could decide not to be agoraphobic. If you suffer from agoraphobia you will know better. You will have tried everything in an effort to lead a normal, happy and relaxed life, yet nothing seems to work. Quite simply, many people are ashamed of being agoraphobic and don't tell anyone about their problem, even those who might be able to help. They try to manage themselves, and they find it very difficult.

On the other hand, they may have sought help from friends, or even from a professional such as their doctor, and found that the help and understanding they needed wasn't forthcoming. The person who should have been able to help considered their problem to be 'not a real illness', to be psychological or mental or in some way to be the fault of the person who was experiencing it. If you have had this experience you will know how painful it can be. Agoraphobia can be a dreadful, lonely condition, with the agoraphobic person feeling cut off even from the people he or she loves and trusts.

There could be many reasons for this, but the most likely explanation is that the person from whom you seek help doesn't really understand the condition and has no idea how to respond.

Or it may be that they do understand it, that they feel anxiety in some situations themselves, and so are threatened by your admission of your agoraphobia. They just don't want to know because it brings out their own uncertainties. There is no greater barrier to help and understanding than plain ignorance.

It is easy to see why there is such lack of understanding. Many people who actually suffer from agoraphobia don't really understand it themselves. It is just an amorphous mass of unpleasant sensations and fears without any logic, defying all explanation, something fearful and something to be hidden, something to run away from. That is why I am trying to show that agoraphobia is a condition which responds to logical explanation, and that it can even be characterized as a physical illness just as real and as tangible as diabetes or asthma.

In some countries doctors consider agoraphobia to be a physical condition, and it is called 'hyperadrenalinaemia', or 'primary hyperventillation syndrome'. Or it may be considered to be a 'psychophysiological' state, a wonderfully complicated word which means that it is both a psychological condition and a physical condition. When we come to discuss in detail the way your symptoms are produced, these terms will have some meaning, but for now let's just remember that agoraphobia is as much a physical condition as it is a psychological one, if not more so. If you think of it in that way you may find it easier to manage.

Phobias

Agora*phobia* is just a phobia, like any other phobia. People are phobic about spiders, about travelling in aircraft or driving on motorways. All phobias have the same characteristics, and the same mechanisms which produce them in the first place and keep them going once they have started. It is a condition in which an idea, or an object or an animal, or a situation, produces real physical symptoms which are severe and threatening. The situation or object isn't in itself dangerous, but it is perceived by our bodies to be dangerous and so our nervous system automatically produces a reaction which would be appropriate for danger, but which is quite inappropriate for the supermarket or the High Street.

Phobias overlap. Claustrophobia is known by all to be a fear of being trapped in a confined space and people understand that, but you can be just as trapped in a supermarket queue. If you are in a crowd on the High Street and you experience the symptoms of panic, where can you go? The panic is in your head and in your body, and you cannot escape from that. It can be a frightening thought.

And so. . . ?

There really is no need to be frightened. I hope that you are already thinking about your agoraphobia in a slightly different way, seeing it as a physical condition which may respond to physical treatment and which is in no way mystifying or frightening. If that is so then we can get on with the business of dealing with it without having to worry about what it is or why you have become agoraphobic, or about what other people might think, and, most important of all, you will know that there is nothing wrong with you apart from your phobia. You aren't different from anyone else. You aren't going mad. There's nothing strange or different about you. You have nothing to hide. If one of those people who may have been sceptical about your condition suddenly suffered your symptoms, they would be terrified, think that they are seriously ill and probably rush to hospital. It is almost certainly true that you face a serious problem with a great deal of courage, and that you should really be proud of the way you manage.

You must have confidence in yourself. You must believe that you can overcome your agoraphobia because it is true, and as you start to deal successfully with your problem your confidence will return. You will prove to yourself that you can deal with your problem by actually doing it. You don't have to take my word for these things, you can prove it to yourself. I would urge you not just to read this book, but also to make time to do the exercises and tasks described and to work hard. Do it in the knowledge and belief that you can get better. It is worth the effort because the reward is great. The reward is nothing more or less than a normal life. That is worth working for.

Points to remember

- The unpleasant sensations you experience in certain situations are real.
- Fear of these sensations is very understandable.
- Agoraphobia could be thought of as an entirely physical condition.
- You can overcome agoraphobia if you go about it the right way.

2

Understanding Agoraphobia

We have some more work to do before we can claim that we really understand agoraphobia, and understand it we must if we are to overcome it. You might think that the study of agoraphobia is a relatively new thing, or that no one really knows very much about it, but you would be wrong.

A man called Bendikt wrote about a condition which he called 'Platzschwindel', or dizziness in public places, in 1870. He thought it was a disorder of the eyes. In 1871 Westphal described many of the symptoms we have already mentioned, including palpitations, blushing, and trembling. He also described the feeling of apprehension, the fear of provoking unwanted attention and the fear of dying. In the same year Cordes pointed out that mental images, thoughts and ideas, could produce the same symptoms and that the condition wasn't just a physical reaction as had been thought. Much has been written since.

Agoraphobia as taboo

Learned people have studied agoraphobia for over a hundred years, and a great deal has been written about it. Why, then, does it often seem that you are the only one to suffer from it? Why do you feel so alone when in fact you have a common and well-understood condition? One study showed that about seventeen people in every hundred suffer from the symptoms of anxiety to an extent which interferes with their everyday lives, and many of those symptoms will be provoked by exposure to public places. Many experienced doctors believe that it is even much more common than that.

The fact that agoraphobia is not talked about says more about the type of society we live in than about the mysteries of the condition. There is still a stigma attached to what are thought of as psychological illnesses. We live in a world of superheroes and we are all supposed to be able to cope with any situation, and to have any disability is thought by some to be a sign of weakness. To have a condition which has no outward signs and which has a psychological element is just too much for some people, and society at large simply closes the door on it.

Many people simply cannot understand the condition, and as a result find it frightening. That also applies to many who suffer from agoraphobia, who may spend years of their lives and a great deal of money trying to find an alternative medical answer to their problems. The first step in treating this condition is to understand it and accept that you are actually suffering from agoraphobia. If you don't really believe in agoraphobia, or if you don't believe that you could suffer from it, if you cannot accept that it is a real and understandable condition, then you have no chance of overcoming it. If you believe that it is really a virus illness which causes your symptoms then you will have great difficulty in treating your condition because you cannot be cured of something you haven't got. So what are the characteristics of agoraphobia?

The characteristics of agoraphobia

How do you know that you have agoraphobia? That may seem an obvious question – if you didn't think that you had agoraphobia you wouldn't be reading this book. Of course, we all know that an agoraphobic person is frightened of open spaces, or as we now prefer to say, experiences unpleasant symptoms in open spaces. That is a rather old-fashioned definition. Is a supermarket an open space? Is an elevator an open space – does a person who experiences symptoms in an elevator suffer from claustrophobia rather than agoraphobia, and at the end of the day does it matter?

The definition of agoraphobia has now widened to include most of the experiences which a person might encounter outside the confines of his or her home. That might be a wide open space such as the top of a mountain, or it might be that supermarket queue, or it might be a theatre, and although agoraphobia is about open spaces there is also an element of confinement. It is not being able to get out of the queue, or the bus, or the bank, *not being in control*, which causes the problem.

Typically the symptoms of agoraphobia get worse the further one gets from a place of safety, such as one's home. The symptoms are reduced by the presence of a trusted companion, or even by a stick or an umbrella. The presence of a child or a dog will help, and many a mother finds taking her toddler to school much easier than the journey back home.

Agoraphobia is made worse by the stress which sometimes accompanies it, and another name for agoraphobia is 'phobic anxiety'. There is often an element of avoidance with agoraphobia, so the sufferer may find that he or she may be avoiding difficult situations.

Then there is the problem of fear. An agoraphobic person doesn't feel in control of his or her body, so there is a fear of becoming conspicuous, of becoming 'disinhibited', which means saying or doing something in public which will attract attention. Another fear is the fear of death or of serious illness, or the fear of fainting or falling down, or of not being able to move, to cross the road or walk across the room.

Another typical problem is that of anticipatory fear. You wake up in the morning feeling apprehensive, and that feeling gets worse as the time to go out approaches. Often the anticipatory fear is worse than the real event, and after you arrive the symptoms of fear diminish. How many of these problems do you recognize? My guess is that if you suffer from agoraphobia you will be familiar with many of them. A woman we will call Sheila certainly was.

Sheila was twenty-two when I first met her. She was a pleasant, intelligent and attractive young woman who was about to get married. She seemed to have everything to live for, and indeed she was extremely happy – apart from one problem. I asked her to tell me about it.

Sheila

The first time I realized that something was wrong was when I

14

was in the theatre. I often go to the theatre but on this occasion I hadn't been feeling very well before I went out. My boyfriend turned up late but as it was a play I particularly wanted to see we decided to go anyway. In the theatre I became very hot and felt flustered, and for some reason I started to think that people were looking at me. It was very frightening. I had an overwhelming urge to just get up and leave, but I stayed, I think because I didn't trust myself to actually walk to the exit. Quite suddenly there was a wave of heat that came right over me. I thought I was going to collapse. My heart was pounding. It was terrible. I managed to wait to the end, and then I felt a bit better. I didn't tell my boyfriend. I didn't know what to say. It was a dreadful experience.

I asked Sheila how she felt normally, whether she had any other problems.

I have been very nervous recently, but then my gran died two weeks ago and I have just put it down to that. I was very close to her and she was looking forward to the wedding. I do feel very panicky a lot of the time now and I'm terrified that this attack might happen again.

Sheila's problems were typical of the sort of thing that many agoraphobic people experience. First of all, agoraphobia sufferers tend to be women in the 18–35 age group. The first event in their problem tends to be sudden, often a sudden anxiety attack, and there is often a background of stress, of bereavement or of financial or marital problems. Despite this background stress, the attack comes out of the blue and it terrifies the person who experiences it.

How do you fit in?

No one experiences all the symptoms we have considered, but many people do have at least some of the features of the condition mentioned above. The onset of the condition may seem to be sudden, but if you think back carefully there will often be problems with anxiety going back for some time, perhaps even years. The background stress, if it is there at all, may be minimal, something you might not even be aware of. You don't have to be a young woman, you might be an elderly man and still suffer from agoraphobia, and the day-to-day profile of your condition might be different.

Just the same, you may well be surprised by just how many of the above symptoms relate to your particular problem. You may now realize that you aren't alone, that many people suffer just the same as you do, and that there is quite a lot known about your condition. It follows that if a lot is known about it, someone must have given a lot of thought about how to deal with it. There are ways of dealing with your particular kind of agoraphobia, and help is at hand. Before getting on to that, we must know something about the dynamics of the condition. Just what is it that happens to you?

The adrenalin reaction

Maybe it's time we had a look at exactly what happened to Sheila in the supermarket. We have spent some time establishing that there is nothing imaginary about our symptoms, that they are real, and that they are powerful. The most frightening and the most powerful physical event associated with agoraphobia is the 'panic attack', or we might call it the 'acute anxiety attack'. Just because it is so powerful and so frightening, we will look at it first and consider other symptoms and problems later.

If you are agoraphobic and have never had one of these attacks don't worry, you probably never will, but they are common and you should know about them anyway. If you have had one, or if you have them frequently, then you will know exactly what I am talking about.

To really understand what happens in one of these attacks you have to know something about how your body works. The study of the working of the body is called 'physiology', and you may remember that agoraphobia was described as a psychophysio-logical condition in Chapter 1, meaning that it is a mixture of psychological and physical occurrences. A panic attack is exactly that – the mental or psychological appreciation of danger followed by a severe physical reaction to that danger. It is just an exaggeration of a normal event and as such it can do you no harm, so the only thing you have to worry about is the unpleasant sensation it produces.

We will talk about why it happens later, but for the moment let's just think about what it is that happens to you in the supermarket, in the street or in a crowd. Just what is this wave of panic? The first thing to say is that most of the workings of your body are controlled automatically. You know nothing about them, and you can do nothing about them. The automatic part of your nervous system takes care of it for you. You don't have to adjust the focus of your eyes, for example. You don't have to ensure that there is a wave of contractions which carries the contents of the intestine from one end to the other. You don't have to control the tension in your muscles consciously when you get out of a chair or walk along. All these things, and many more, are controlled automatically by your automatic nervous system.

Your automatic nervous system serves you very well. It helps you in all sorts of ways. If you want to cross a road you don't have to compute the speeds of all passing vehicles and the width of the road – your automatic nervous system will do all of that for you and you will know that it is safe to cross. If you are half way across the road and a car careers towards you out of control, your body will tell you that you are in danger, and your body will respond to that danger without your having to consciously do anything. You will have extra strength and extra power, your pulse will speed up and you will have extra sugar released into your bloodstream so that you can run or jump faster or higher than you would have believed possible. If you are confronted by danger your body reacts, and this is called the 'fight or flight' reaction. You have extra strength to fight that enemy or, perhaps more sensibly, more strength to run away.

All this is very well, but what happens if your body gets it wrong? What happens if you get this flight or fight reaction in situations which aren't really dangerous, and in situations where you can't run away? I'm sure you've guessed the answer to that question – you have a panic attack. What happens is that your automatic nervous system misinterprets your surroundings and for some reason perceives them as being dangerous, and it sounds the alarm bells – but it is a false alarm. At the same time it releases its emergency response, a substance called adrenalin, into your bloodstream. All you are aware of is that feeling of heat, of your pulse racing, of being sweaty, all things which you wouldn't be aware of if you were running away. It is an entirely normal response experienced in an inappropriate situation.

Why should your body release a substance into your bloodstream in times of danger? Why should it choose this particular mechanism for tuning up your system? The answer is that your response to danger is very comprehensive, involving all sorts of different organs. It diverts blood from the peripheries to the muscles and it releases stored sugar from the liver, and these various effects cannot be achieved by simple impulses sent down your nerves, but as your blood reaches all parts of your body, a substance in the blood can affect all parts and functions of the body instantaneously. It is really very clever.

Adrenalin is released by the adrenal glands, two tiny glands situated one above each kidney. Each has a nerve supply, and when stimulated by that nerve it releases its adrenalin with the results already described. If that adrenalin is suddenly released, you have either the flight or fight reaction if it is an appropriate release for real danger, or possibly a panic attack if you are in that supermarket queue. But what happens if there is just a little too much adrenalin being released over a long period of time?

In that case there isn't the sudden onset of symptoms as in a panic attack, there is the slow onset of symptoms which are less dramatic but equally distressing. You may be in a public place and feeling uncomfortable without knowing why. It is just that you have too much circulating adrenalin which is producing symptoms which make you feel uncomfortable. It is all very straightforward and logical. There is no mystery about the adrenalin reaction, it is a simple physiological response common to everyone. It is unfortunate that in your case it has got a little out of control.

It is worth mentioning that there is one other mechanism which can produce some of the symptoms you experience in public places, and that is over-breathing. It doesn't have to be obvious over-breathing, taking big gasps or panting, it may just be the fact that you are breathing a little too deeply without even being aware of it yourself, a situation we call 'hyperventilation'. When you over-breathe in this way you blow off carbon dioxide and that changes your blood chemistry and so produces symptoms. These symptoms are mostly tightness in muscles, and you may feel dizzy and ill as well.

Again this is a normal condition rather than an illness. There is nothing wrong with your body. If anyone over-breathed they would experience the same sensations. If anyone were confronted by a stressful experience they would put out adrenalin and experience the same sensations you experience. There is nothing wrong with the functioning of the body of someone who suffers from agoraphobia, they experience the same things which anyone can experience, but they may experience them in unusual situations or they may experience them more severely. It is a matter of degree.

Why does this happen to you? Why should your automatic nervous system turn on so easily? Why should it do so in public places? Why are the symptoms you experience so powerful and so frightening? It's almost as if your body has turned against you. It is a serious business and you might even be close to despair. Just because your symptoms are natural and explicable doesn't make them any less severe, less disturbing or less disruptive. They may be so powerful that you have become almost housebound. You may now know something about the mechanisms which are causing your symptoms but that doesn't mean that you can control them. You may know something about how they work, but nothing about why they happen, and that is more important. In the next chapter we will go on to consider your symptoms in more detail, and to think about how they have developed.

Points to remember

- Symptoms are produced by too much adrenalin in your circulation.
- Everyone can experience the same symptoms.
- Slight over-breathing can also produce symptoms.
- An agoraphobic person gets symptoms more easily than someone else.
- An agoraphobic person gets symptoms in different situations than someone else.

3

Making a Start

We have come quite a distance down the road towards understanding the problem of agoraphobia, and we have seen that
there is nothing mysterious about it. There are still questions to
be asked, of course, not least of which is why we have come to see
crowds or open spaces as being dangerous. We do know,
however, that our body's response to that perceived danger is
entirely normal, if a little extreme. We will consider these
problems later, but for now I hope that we have 'demystified'
many of the frightening elements of your agoraphobia and that
you will be able to think positively about the possibility of
overcoming your problem. There is, however, a catch.

The catch

The catch is this: no matter how well you understand everything
about your agoraphobia, no matter how simple it seems, you will
not be able to deal with the problem simply by *understanding* it.
This is extremely frustrating. You know what your problem is,
you know why you feel the way you do, you know how your body
works, but even so you cannot stop the sensations from
happening.

An intellectual appreciation of the problem of agoraphobia is
a start, but by itself it won't help. There are ways of dealing with
the problem and I will tell you about them, but reading this book
is not enough by itself. It's like joining a gym in order to get fit.
Just joining the gym won't do it, you actually have to go to the
gym and do the exercises, and it's the same with the exercises in
this book. You have to make a commitment to actually doing
them, and if you do that you will certainly overcome your
agoraphobia.

Don't believe anyone who tells you that they can cure your
agoraphobia – they can't. Only *you* can do that. But it isn't that

difficult, certainly no more so than going to the gym to get fit or to lose weight. You need a bit of determination, and you have to make time, but you can do that. You can and must do it because the rewards for so doing are great, nothing more or less than achieving an entirely normal lifestyle, learning to enjoy your life again, and achieving fulfilment.

Making a start

The secret of overcoming the problem of agoraphobia is to break it down into its constituents, to make it manageable, and then to deal with the different parts one at a time. Overcoming agoraphobia is a straightforward demolition job, but you have to knock the bricks out of the wall one at a time.

Initially when your agoraphobia starts it is just a frightening mass of feelings and reactions with no form. As time goes by you get to know it, whether you like it or not. You know what is likely to happen and where it will happen, and as a result you begin to avoid the situations which produce your symptoms – avoidance behaviour is something we will talk about later because it is very important. What you have to do now is to start to use this information to your own advantage. Overcoming your agoraphobia is like a game of chess, and like a game of chess it can be enjoyable. At the end of the day you will know more about yourself.

We have already made a start, of course. Just reading this book is a start because it indicates a desire to get to grips with your problem, and that is essential if you are to succeed. Understanding the nature of the problem, knowing that it is a common problem, realizing that many other people also suffer from it, believing that there is nothing wrong with your mind or body, all these concepts are necessary if you are to succeed in your task. What is required now is a little work.

Keeping a diary

If your agoraphobia has built a wall between you and the rest of the world, that wall will have to be demolished. It may well be a very substantial wall and if you are to succeed you will have to knock out one brick at a time until the entire edifice crumbles. These bricks are the symptoms you experience and the small events which recharge your phobia, and if you are going to deal with them you have to identify them first. You can't demolish your wall right away, you have to reduce it to its smallest components and deal with each in turn. But how do you do that?

If you wish to overcome an enemy you first have to know your enemy, and we have begun that process. You know about the adrenalin reaction and how it works, how it causes physical symptoms, and now you must look at your own problems and see how the adrenalin reaction effects you. You have to be precise and accurate. It's no good saying that you just don't feel well in a public place, or that you don't like going into a particular place or even that you're scared to go into a threatening situation. You can't deal with something which is amorphous and diffuse because you can't really define what it is. You have to nail your problem down so that it can't move and then you have something you can deal with. Carve it up with the precision of a surgeon into tiny pieces and you can brush them aside. If you want to do that you need a pencil and paper.

Writing things down helps to make them concrete and therefore vulnerable to attack. You now have to devise a system for recording your problems so that you can define them. You need to keep a diary. It doesn't have to be a great book, a sheet of writing paper or the back of an envelope will do. The important thing is to make a note of the way you feel or, even better, the symptoms you experience at all times during a given week. Write down what day it is, divide the day into morning, afternoon and evening, and then write down what you are doing at any given time, and what symptoms you experience. Say whether they are mild, moderate, severe or very severe. It is important that you do it at the time as your recollection may be inaccurate. This is your first task and it is important that you do it properly because it is the first step on your ladder to success, and if you are to progress you have to have laid the groundwork.

A typical diary would read as follows. It was kept by a young woman called Marianne who had agoraphobia.

Marianne's Diary

	MORNING	AFTERNOON	EVENING
Mon	*Have to take Tina and Tony to school. Hate Mondays. Feel sick before breakfast. Diarrhoea. Shaky getting kids ready. (Moderately bad.) Get palpitations leaving house but settle down. Go by Dale Street to avoid other people. Gets worse as we move further away from house. Tummy cramps. (Bad.) Talk to children. Leave kids off and feel sick. Head for home. Don't look at anyone because would break down if had to speak.*	*Stay in house. Have to pick up kids so it is repeat performance except coming home easier. Severe headache. Wait for Mike to come in. He is understanding as always and I feel much better.*	*Stay in. Watch TV.*
Tues	*Same as Mon. (Maybe not so bad.)*	*Repeat in the afternoon but feeling very tense due to shopping this evening. Feel dizzy in the house (severe). Cry when Mike comes in.*	*Late night shopping as usual. Pace up and down hall. Into bathroom three or four times (diarrhoea). Tremor (severe). Trouble breathing in the car but manage. Mike holds my arm and I hang on to the trolley. Thank*

24

	MORNING	AFTERNOON	EVENING
			goodness not busy. Tearful and trembly. Keep an eye on the exit. Mike gets most of the stuff and does the queue while I wait. Seems to take for ever. Feel more relaxed now that it's almost over. Much better in car home. Very tired.
Wed	*Have to go to post office after leaving children off. Walk about until it should be quiet. Queue when I go in. Should have walked out but didn't. More people came in, all friendly and cheerful. Felt panic building up (very severe). Thought I might shout out but didn't. HAD PANIC ATTACK (terrible). Left post office and went home as fast as possible. Felt better at home. Cried.*	*Arranged for mother to pick up children. Waited for Mike. Seeing doctor tomorrow . . .*	

This is clearly the diary of a very ill young woman. Her agoraphobia was on the point of making her housebound, so her decision to seek help was very timely. It was keeping a diary which showed just how severe her problem had become, and it was her diary which helped her to overcome it. It was an important first step.

There is a very real reason for taking a lot of time and trouble over your diary because it is the basis of your own treatment plan. You must know exactly what it is that happens to you, and where it is that it happens. You have to start unravelling the strands of your problem. Don't write too much, you have to have something you can read and use easily, but do make a record of the things that happen to you.

Why do we get symptoms?

Let's take a look at the symptoms recorded in Marianne's diary. Here is a list:

Feeling sick
Diarrhoea } before leaving the house
Tremor
Palpitations

Tummy cramps } going to school
Feeling sick

Headache
Tenseness, muscle pains in shoulders } at home
Dizziness
Diarrhoea

Trouble breathing } in the car

Feeling of wanting to shout out } at the post office
Panic attack

If you suffer from agoraphobia you may well recognize some of these unpleasant symptoms. Some of them may well appear in your diary, though you may record others as well. You know that they are caused by an excess of the substance adrenalin which is released into your bloodstream. But why are so many apparently different symptoms produced?

We know that the function of adrenalin in nature is to tone the body up in every conceivable way to make it fit for action, but that doesn't explain the variety of symptoms you experience. The answer is that adrenalin affects different organs in different

26

ways, as we have already explained, so a great variety of different symptoms are produced when the system is overacting. There is, however, a logical explanation to everything which happens to you, as we will now see. Let's consider a quite arbitrary list of symptoms which were recorded in a survey done in my own practice:

Panic Attacks

Many people who suffer from agoraphobia experience, or have experienced, panic attacks in public places. They often occur when the individual feels trapped, often in a queue or in theatre or cinema at a quiet time when they feel conspicuous. It is a very frightening experience, particularly the first time it happens, and you may even feel that you are going to faint or die. In fact nothing serious happens or can happen because a panic attack is simply the sudden release of adrenalin into the bloodstream and the sensations that it produces are just an exaggeration of many other symptoms. It comes on quickly, and goes away just as quickly. If you can stay where you are and breathe quietly the attack will soon be over and you can carry on as usual. If you are good at doing this an observer need never know that you have had a panic attack.

Pain

An agoraphobic person tends to be physically tense, and indeed such a person often has an anxious type of personality. By 'tense' we mean that the muscles are tense and tight, and that can produce pain. It may be chest pain from cramping muscles in your chest wall, or neck pain, or pain almost anywhere. In difficult situations over-breathing can produce painful cramps.

Headache

Head pain often comes from the neck, and anxious people tend to have tense muscles, as we have said. If you are anxious in some situations you may have neck or head pain, and you can test it by pressing on the muscles of your neck with your thumb. If that makes your pain worse then you know that it is the tension in your neck muscles which is causing your headache.

Muscle tension

Muscle tension is caused by too much adrenalin in your circulation, or by over-breathing. It may give you sore muscles anywhere, and the muscles will be sore and tight if you press on them, and you might feel stiff when you walk.

Breathing difficulty

In difficult situations people with agoraphobia often feel that they can't get a full breath, that they have to fight for air. It is the same story, tightness in the muscles which join the ribs together. Fighting for breath makes it worse. We will consider how you can deal with this later.

Swallowing difficulty

You should be beginning to see a pattern to your symptoms now, because swallowing difficulties felt by some people in public places are due to tightness in the throat muscles. You become aware of your swallowing and feel you have to do it more and more, and your muscles begin to cramp. It can be distressing but it isn't dangerous.

Tearfulness

If you feel tearful in public places, feel that you are going to break down, don't worry, you won't. Man's urge to conform is stronger than this type of tearfulness, which isn't to do with sadness or depression, more to do with desperation and with tightness in the muscles of the face. You will find that your teeth are clamped together and your eyes tight and sore. It's almost as if the tears are being squeezed out.

Diarrhoea

This isn't the same type of diarrhoea as one gets with a bowel infection. It's more what we call 'intestinal hurry', or 'frequent loose stools'. It is brought on by 'nerves', by an interview or having to make a speech, and everyone will have experienced it. For someone with agoraphobia, every outing is stressful and so this type of diarrhoea is common. It is caused by the direct action of adrenalin on the muscles of the bowel.

Excessive fatigue

This is something you might experience after you have been tense for some time, and it is just tiredness. Some people who are habitually tense do feel very tired, and this is due to the fact that they do not relax even during sleep, so that they wake up tired and after a time this builds up and the tiredness can become overwhelming. It is really a side-effect of agoraphobia.

Tremor

Close your fist and hold it closed as tightly as possible. Does your hand and arm shake? If your muscles are tight they will shake and you will notice a tremor. It is part of being tense and it will be worse before and during threatening experiences.

Dizziness

There can be all sorts of different causes for dizziness. Some people might describe a panic attack as dizziness, but the dizziness which most agoraphobic people complain of is a feeling of instability, a feeling that they are falling to the side. If you have this feeling, press on the muscles of your neck and you may find that they are sore and tight on one side. Your neck muscles are involved in your appreciation of balance, and this inequality of the tone in the muscles of your neck produces the feeling of instability or dizziness.

Palpitations

These are extra heartbeats. There is an extra beat and then a gap, and it is often the gap that you notice as a funny feeling in your chest. There is nothing wrong with your heart, it is just the result of too much adrenalin which can alter your heart rate and make it put in this extra beat or beats. It is very common and will do you no harm.

Stomach discomfort

Too much adrenalin means too much acid, so you can have the feelings of indigestion or sickness. You may also experience 'stomach cramps'; these occur for the same reason as the diarrhoea you may sometimes have. Adrenalin makes the bowel overwork and cause spasms in the bowel muscles, and these are painful. You may also experience distension of your abdomen.

Why pay so much attention to symptoms?

You might think that getting too concerned about the physical sensations you experience would make you preoccupied with the physical problems you may have, and that is a risk you take, but there are benefits which far outweigh the risks. You have to give your agoraphobia some form, and it may be that you haven't previously considered the physical side of the condition. You have just been aware that you are feeling terrible, and now you want to know in what way you feel terrible.

If you understand the mechanisms which are causing you such misery the problem is 'demystified', made more understandable, and the discomfort becomes explicable. It gives you the opportunity for working on individual symptoms, and that is something we will discuss at length. Each individual symptom can be made easier using simple techniques, and you can work on individual symptoms when you cannot work on 'agoraphobia' as an entity in itself.

There is another reason, perhaps the most important reason, and that is that it raises to a level of consciousness something which is now automatic, which is a physical habit, something which just happens without your being aware of it. It is only by making yourself aware of the things which happen to your body that you can begin to make inroads in your problem, and starting with your symptoms is the most practical way there is to get going. If you become aware of the physical symptoms you experience you begin to notice them earlier, so that you can begin to deal with them earlier and as a result have some chance of overcoming them. Once your agoraphobia has got going it is very difficult to deal with it.

Begin now

You have to make a start. You must do the work or you will not succeed in overcoming your problem, and it is a problem which can be overcome. What is worse, it is a problem that might become more difficult to deal with as you get older. The ways of dealing with your problem may seem simplistic, but they work if you use them, and when you start to deal with your problem you will feel better just because you are doing something – so make a start. Keep your diary for one week, and longer if the week you choose is not representative of your average week. You might find the results interesting.

Points to remember

- Keeping a symptom diary is a first step.
- Your agoraphobia is made up of a collection of symptoms.
- Your symptoms have simple physical explanations.
- You can deal with your problem if you tackle it one step at a time.

4

The Tricks of the Trade

If you suffer from agoraphobia you will be very keen to get on with the task of overcoming it, and we will now look at techniques which you will find useful in achieving this end. Just the same, it is important that we don't move too fast, that each step is considered and taken carefully. It is also helpful, indeed essential, that you understand the true nature of agoraphobia, why it happens and how it works. If you are going to beat this problem, you have to know what you are doing. Before learning about the tools you can use, let's ask, and attempt to answer, a few questions.

Who suffers from agoraphobia?

Psychologists have considered this question for years, and much research has been carried out and many theories have been propounded. A particular personality type has been thought to be susceptible – the 'dependent personality', someone with domineering parents and little will of their own. This concept will not please many people who suffer from agoraphobia who know that they have strong personalities and who battle against their complaint every day with great courage.

I think that this concept is nonsense. In my experience of people who have this condition, there is no stereotype. Anyone can have agoraphobia, from the boardroom down to the cleaners. You can be of any personality type, any height, weight, colour, or creed. It can happen to anyone. Anyone can develop a condition where they experience symptoms when they even consider leaving their house, and it often seems that this agoraphobia is somehow 'tacked on' to their other personality. They can be of any type, but the added agoraphobia is always essentially the same, just like any other illness.

It is often said that someone *is* agoraphobic, but it would be more accurate to say that they *suffer from* agoraphobia, implying that their essential personality is exactly the same as it was before they developed their agoraphobia. I suppose that people with diabetes or asthma might take exception to being called diabetic or asthmatic, but there aren't the same psychological implications to a physical condition such as theirs. Once you get rid of your agoraphobia you will be exactly the same person as you were before you developed your agoraphobia. You will just be older and wiser.

Is agoraphobia more common in young women?

This is another myth. One possible reason for the myth is that young women are more in contact with their doctors for other medical reasons, so that their agoraphobia is more likely to be reported. Men and women of all ages suffer from agoraphobia, though men may be more reluctant to admit the fact in this macho world. There is nothing which predisposes women to the condition, and no age group is immune.

Do agoraphobic people tend to be anxious?

This is certainly true. Agoraphobia doesn't exist in isolation, and people who suffer from it tend to have a higher incidence of 'free-floating', or more generalized anxiety. That is really saying that they have their agoraphobic symptoms at other times as well as when they are in public. They can feel anxious at home or at quiet times as well, but their anxiety symptoms are worse in crowded places. They may also have other phobias, and remember that agora*phobia* is merely one particular phobia, and an anxious person may have other quite unrelated phobias. In some cases it is hard to draw the line between generalized anxiety and anxiety which happens to be worse in certain situations.

The most important thing to know and to remember is that agoraphobia can be overcome, and that it can be overcome using the methods described in this book. That has been proven, and the theories about which type of person may develop agoraphobia or why they develop it are incidental. No matter how severe your agoraphobia may be, and no matter how long you may have had your problem, it can be overcome, but if you are to overcome it you will need some 'tools of the trade' to help you. If you are to find out about them you first have to look at the diary you have been keeping.

Your diary

The ability to keep a usable diary is the first skill you need, as your diary is an excellent tool which can be used in many different ways. If you have been keeping a diary, you will have a list of your own symptoms. I will use the list of symptoms from the previous chapter:

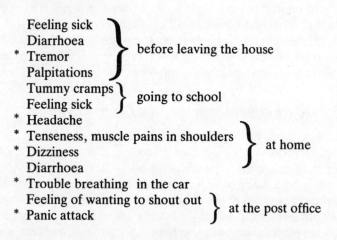

Muscle tension, actual tightness in the muscles, is a major cause of six of these thirteen symptoms, and it contributes most of the others. I have indicated them with an asterisk so you can count them yourself. It also causes the excessive tiredness which many anxious people feel because they don't get enough relaxed sleep, and it is the tension in your muscles which may cause you the greatest discomfort in public places and which may give you other feelings such as the sensation that you might fall. It is one of the things which makes you feel insecure in public. Look at your own list of symptoms and situations and see how important the actual tightness of your muscles may be to you.

Muscle tension and relaxation

Most people know about the importance of relaxation in dealing with such problems as stress, but relaxation is fundamental to the management of many similar problems and that includes agoraphobia. Muscle tightness is the common factor in any psychological condition which has physical manifestations. If you are in any doubt about the importance of muscle tension to you, the next time you are in a public place and feeling uncomfortable, push your thumb into the muscles of your neck and see just how sore they are. All the muscles in your body will be tight and sore. Why do they get like that, and why can't you relax them?

Your muscles get tight because of the action of adrenalin, or through over-breathing, and you can't relax them because you can't turn off the adrenalin. Muscle tension can become a habit, and if you are habitually tense you simply aren't able to relax your muscles. If you wake up in the morning feeling stiff and sore, with a painful neck and shoulders, a tight jaw and nail marks in the palms of your hands from clenching your fists all night, you simply cannot *choose* not to be tense – you must actively do something to control it.

If you suffer from agoraphobia, you will be tense in public places, on public transport or in theatres, often unbearably and certainly uncontrollably so. You really can do nothing about it – *unless you have learned the skill of relaxation*. You have to learn how to relax actively, and you can do that in privacy in your own home. When you have learned the skill, then you can use it in public places without anyone knowing.

Relaxation isn't the answer to all of your problems, but it is a tool you can use, and it is a start. It helps to put you back in control of your body, and that is important because at the moment it is often your body which is controlling your life.

Relaxation exercises

The most important thing about relaxation exercises is actually to do them. It is easy to read them through and think 'Right, I know that', and actually do nothing. Do them now, or as soon as possible, and take them seriously. Remember that you are learning a technique which you can later use anywhere, and that you have to perfect this technique and become expert in its use.

Make sure you have privacy, and that you have a warm room in which to practise. Either lie on a bed or, better, sit in a good chair with your head supported. Make sure that you are comfortable. Play music if you like and try to relax for a moment or two. Either close your eyes or else fix your eyes on an object or mark on a wall of the room, then begin the exercises. Don't expect to succeed right away, treat this as an exercise which you will have to perfect.

Begin by squeezing your right fist. Tighten it up. Hold it tight for a few seconds. Now relax it suddenly. Feel the relaxation come into your arm right up to your shoulder, like a feeling of warmth passing up your arm. Notice and enjoy that feeling of relaxation. Now go to your left hand. Make a fist and tighten it up, hold that for a few seconds and then relax it suddenly. Feel and enjoy the feeling of relaxation in your arm and shoulder. Slow your breathing and let your whole body relax.

Now pull your shoulders up and hold them up for a few seconds. Now suddenly relax them, letting your shoulders and arms hang loose. Feel the relaxation coming into your shoulders and neck. Enjoy that feeling, slow your breathing and continue to breathe slowly and deeply letting your whole body relax.

Now it's time to move on to your neck. It is often your neck which is most stiff and tense and may be the most difficult part to relax. Push your neck back and hold it there. Tighten your neck muscles and hold them tight for a moment. Now relax them suddenly and enjoy that feeling of relaxation. Breathe slowly in through your nose and out through your mouth. You should aim to get your breathing rate down to about eight breaths per minute.

Next tighten up your facial muscles. Make a frown. Clench your teeth tightly and wrinkle your forehead. Hold that, then quickly relax the muscles and slow your breathing as before, enjoying the sensation of relaxation in your face and throughout your body.

Move on to your stomach. Pull in your tummy and make yourself as slim as possible, and hold that position. Hold it and then relax your stomach muscles suddenly, slowing your breathing. Just let your whole body loosen up and relax, and slow your breathing right down. When you are comfortable, arch your back and hold that position, with your back muscles tight. Hold that and then relax it, going through the same procedures as before.

Lastly it is the turn of your legs. Push the toes of both feet away from you and stretch your legs, tightening up the muscles. Don't hold it too long or you might get cramp in your legs and that would spoil everything. Suddenly relax your legs and enjoy the feeling of relaxation, slow your breathing right down, and let your body go loose.

You have now almost finished the exercise. You have been slowing your breathing down during the exercise, and you should stay where you are and continue to slow your breathing until you have reduced it to a rate of about eight breaths a minute. This will increase your feeling of relaxation. Don't expect to be able to achieve total relaxation straight away – you may still feel a little tense. It takes time and daily practice, but when you have achieved real relaxation you will know. You will feel warm and comfortable, almost as if you are floating, and this is a very pleasant sensation for a habitually tense person.

Continue your relaxation sessions by thinking warm relaxing thoughts. Think about a warm beach or warm luxurious bed. Think 'relaxation'. Think 'slow down', 'take it easy'. When you feel that you have done enough, count down: 'three, two, one, wake up'. Now you are back in the real world. You may feel relaxed and refreshed, but that is not really the point of your session. You are learning a technique which you will be able to use anywhere. That is what it is all about. You have to be able to take it out with you whenever you have to face a difficult situation and use it.

Difficulties

There are some obvious difficulties about learning relaxation, and you may be disappointed by the results at first. You may find that you simply cannot relax. You may find that you can relax, but when you finish your exercises and stand up you are as tense as ever and your relaxation doesn't last. That is all right. You can't expect to learn to relax and to stay relaxed right away. These are techniques you have to practise over and over again.

It may help to make a tape-recording of your own voice saying the exercises as you do them. Make sure that you allow enough time, and allow time at the beginning for you to get settled before you start. Most of all, keep working at the exercises.

Alternatively, you may relax too well and fall asleep. That doesn't help much, and you may have to use a tape-recording of your own voice to aid your concentration and simply try to stay awake. You can, of course, use these exercises to get you off to sleep at night, and that can be helpful. A young patient of mine whom we will call Jennifer learned relaxation techniques from me and when she came back to report her progress she told me that she had had some difficulties.

Jennifer

The relaxation exercises were great, but they weren't easy. It was difficult to make the time for even the first session. It was difficult to explain to my husband just what I was doing by myself, and I certainly felt a little strange going off to the bedroom to just sit in a chair. Every day there seemed to be other things which were more important which I should have been doing. At first I couldn't relax at all and it just seemed a waste of time, but on the third day I really got it right, and the feeling was terrific. It was like lying in a warm bath, but as soon as I got out of the chair I was just as tense as ever, and as I had just been relaxed it seemed worse than it ever was. I'm trying to stay relaxed after the session for longer by just staying in the chair. Still, I've kept at it and I can do it every time now, and I'm trying to use it in the car. It's very difficult, but I can see that if I keep practising it will make a big difference. The real difficulty is keeping at it. I missed the session on Thursday and had to try hard to remember to do it on Friday. You could get out of the habit very easily.

Jennifer came back to see me regularly, mostly so that I could encourage her to keep doing her relaxation exercises. Keeping at it is by far the most difficult thing, and one way for you to do it is to keep a relaxation diary and make a note of each session, and of just how successful you have been, giving each session a score from 1 to 5. If you start missing days it will be obvious straight away.

Another way to keep at it is to tell someone close to you what you are doing and how important it is, and ask them to help you by giving you encouragement when you do it, and telling you off when you don't. If that person is tense, and many people are, they might want to learn the exercises too, or you might join a relaxation group or a yoga group. It doesn't matter what exercises you do, so long as you do something.

Breathing

Control of your breathing is also very important. The act of over-breathing will in itself make you feel tense and agitated, but over-breathing does more than that. When you over-breathe you blow off carbon dioxide from your lungs, and this changes your blood chemistry by making your blood less acid. This change in your blood produces real effects which include dilated pupils, cold fingers and toes, sweaty palms and armpits, a rapid heart rate and of course, muscle tightness. If you over-breathe, you don't feel very well.

By over-breathing we don't mean hysterical breathing, taking big gasps or breathing very fast. You can achieve some of these unpleasant symptoms by just breathing a little more deeply than you need to, and some people develop the habit of doing just that. They may also sigh frequently, or feel that they need an extra breath from time to time. These things will make you feel panicky and tense, and you should do something about it. Even if you don't tend to over-breathe in normal situations, it is well worth while practising breathing exercises because you may well find that you over-breathe in some difficult situations, and if you can control that, you will feel better. Learning to control your breathing isn't difficult.

Breathing exercises

You don't have to go away by yourself to practise breathing exercises. In fact, they are best done while watching television, but before you start you have to understand a little about the way you breathe.

When you are at rest, you breathe with your diaphragm and the muscles in your chest don't move at all. It is only when you are hurrying or exercising that your chest heaves up and down. When you are relaxed it is your abdomen which moves. You can test this by sitting comfortably, preferably in a reclining position, and placing one hand on your abdomen and the other on your chest. It should be your abdomen hand which moves up and down, and your chest hand should not move at all. If your chest hand moves, you are over-breathing.

The actual breathing exercise is easy. You simply do the above, but stay in that position concentrating on breathing with your abdomen. Notice if you sigh, or if you breathe quickly, and just try to slow things down and get your breathing more regular and relaxed. Make a habit of controlling your breathing when you are quiet at home because you will want to be able to control your breathing when you are outside, and that is more difficult.

Don't become preoccupied with your breathing. Just become aware of the fact that it is something you should be interested in and try to keep it under control as part of your relaxation programme. If you are aware of your breathing it will take care of itself, and that is what you want to achieve.

Is it worth the effort?

These exercises certainly do take a lot of effort, and that effort is worth it for various reasons. The first and most obvious reason is that it gives you tools which you can use against the symptoms which your agoraphobia produces. It means that when you are out and you begin to feel unwell, there *is* something you can do. You don't have to just grin and bear it, you can actually start to deal with the problem, and that makes you feel good. You cease to be the victim, the passive recipient of everything which your body can throw at you. You can start to take control.

The other reason is more subtle, and it follows on from all that has been said about your symptoms. You may remember that we spent a lot of time thinking about your agoraphobia in terms of symptoms so that you could raise to the level of consciousness something which was previously happening quite unconsciously. Being aware of what was happening to you was a start. If you learn to be relaxed and to breathe slowly, you will become aware of when you are becoming tense and when you are over-breathing sooner than you otherwise would, so that you can deal with the problem sooner and defuse the situation before it gets out of hand and takes over. Again it is putting you in control.

Learning these techniques is a start, and it is a start you can make in your own home where you feel safe. What we have to do now is to think about how we can get out of the security of your own home and learn to deal with the real world.

Points to remember

- Learning to relax and breathe is an important first step.
- You can use relaxation and breathing techniques when you are in difficult situations.
- Relaxation techniques help to put you back in charge.
- Learning to relax helps you to realize when you are becoming tense.

5

How Agoraphobia Works

It is surely very strange that the world can be such a threatening place. It seems as if everyone else wanders through various situations without any problems at all, and yet someone who suffers from the effects of agoraphobia can feel isolated and terrified in exactly those situations which others actively enjoy.

Everyone's agoraphobia is different. For some people it is impossible to go out at all, for others it is one particular situation or one aspect of a situation which is difficult or which may even seem impossible. The difference between the comfortable, relaxed person and the tense, phobic person is like the difference between night and day, and it may seem to the agoraphobic person that no one could ever understand his or her problems or imagine what it is like to be on the brink of total breakdown. It may seem that you live in a different world, a strange world, and that you will never enter that other, normal world again.

People's perception of the world is built on misconceptions. For a start, while it may be true that there are people who have no idea what it is like to get symptoms of apprehension and nervousness in public, they are few and far between. Most people have been terrified in one situation or other. They may have had to make a speech, or to ask a girl for a date, or climb to a height, or to face an angry dog if they are fearful of dogs. Very few people are without some sort of phobia. Phobic feelings are things which most people know about and have experience of, but they are not things which are discussed and you don't know what other people may suffer in some situations. After all, do other people know what you suffer?

There is a great urge of conform. It's part of our social behaviour, and we are social animals, so people don't break down in public or show their feelings. Those are things that they keep private, but it's safe to assume that such experiences are common because phobias, or phobic reactions, are essential not only for the survival of our species but for all other species.

Phobias

The 'flight or fight' reaction, which we have already mentioned, has kept our ancestors out of the jaws of predators over the generations. The ability to perceive danger and react to it automatically is built into our physiology – who doesn't know a dog that doesn't run and hide from the crack of a firework, or a horse that doesn't shy at a paper bag or a manhole cover? Animals depend on these automatic reactions more than we do, so they have their phobias, too. The fact is that phobic reactions are not as difficult to understand as they seem. The only thing which is difficult to understand is how we come to perceive certain quite ordinary situations as being threatening.

Even that isn't too difficult to understand. We don't live in an entirely physical world populated by carnivorous dinosaurs. Our survival depends on different things, and running away is no longer as essential for our survival as it was. We have an intellectual concept of the world, and our dangers can be intellectual or psychological, and ideas can be more threatening than real situations. We should never be embarrassed by our phobias. They are logical and they are understandable, and a phobia about exposing ourselves to the real or perceived dangers of a busy public place is quite logical. It may be that if you had lived in the past, you would not have been a fearless hunter, but you might have been a survivor and that might have been more important. One thing is certain, you are still a survivor. You have been up until now, and you will continue to be one.

How does a phobia develop?

Understanding how a phobia develops is essential to understanding how it can be overcome. A phobic reaction is learned, not in a conscious way, but by our bodies as a physical reaction to a stress. How do we come to identify a supermarket as a stressful situation? That is more difficult to explain, but it seems that our 'fight or flight' reaction is triggered by some small event, some unpleasantness, something which gets our adrenalin going. Maybe by coincidence there are several such events, perhaps occurring at a time when we are stressed and our adrenalin is already flowing and our threshold of arousal for the adrenalin reaction is low. We then associate the adrenalin reaction with that situation, and anticipate that we will feel bad in that situation. We fear the symptoms we will experience in the situation, and that fear produces more symptoms. We have developed the phobic 'downward spiral'.

A phobia is a learned phenomenon, and we can represent the way we learn to develop symptoms using the following diagram. We can see how a bad experience can lead to a worse reaction until we are sucked down into a vortex from which it seems impossible to escape. Yet a spiral can be turned the other way, it can become an upward spiral, and that is what we are in the

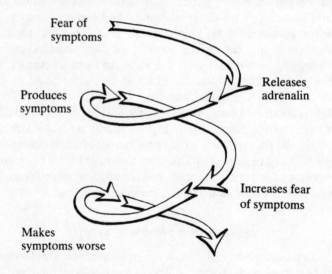

Fear of symptoms

Releases adrenalin

Produces symptoms

Increases fear of symptoms

Makes symptoms worse

process of doing. You can see how one thing leads to another, how a bad experience leads to the production of adrenalin and how that automatically and irrevocably makes the next experience of the same situation worse.

The way forward

Clearly you have to grasp this situation, take control of it and make it work for you instead of against you as it has been doing, and the key to this lies in the fact that your adrenalin reaction is a learned reaction. Your body has simply been learning the wrong lessons. Your reaction to any threatening situation is a conditioned reaction, a 'knee-jerk' response over which you have no control – at the moment. This automatic reaction has been learned by your body in the way shown by our downward spiral diagram, but if a reaction can be learned, surely it can be 'unlearned'? Of course it can.

What we need to do now is to start a process of re-education. We have to teach our automatic nervous system to react in a more acceptable way, and we have to do that consciously and deliberately. It has learned the wrong responses by a series of subliminal reactions of which we have not been aware. How can we start to turn things around? How can we create a situation where we can walk into a party, or into a sports stadium or a supermarket, or just walk down a street, feeling relaxed and comfortable, at ease with our surroundings?

In fact we have already made a start. Much of what we have already discussed has been working towards that end. Your diary, your relaxation and breathing exercises all had as one of their aims the raising of part of your problem to a conscious level. If you have been working at these exercises you will be beginning to notice when you get symptoms, and when you get tense and what it is that makes you uncomfortable.

Things are not happening automatically any more, and if you are taking your breathing and relaxation exercises seriously you will be beginning to be able to use them to control your symptoms in threatening situations. If you reduce the impact of your symptoms at all, even by a little, you are slowing the twist of the spiral and beginning to exert a little control.

The idea is not to suddenly get rid of your symptoms, it is to reduce their severity and thus to gain confidence. If you become more confident, that will reduce the impact of your symptoms, and if you are confident you will perform better in public situations, and that will improve your confidence and then that will reduce your symptoms. Can you see that we can turn the downward spiral the other way, travelling upwards instead of downwards? Before doing that let's have another look at the downward spiral, this time adding the other factors which make our problem worse. We will flesh out the spiral and look at the full picture.

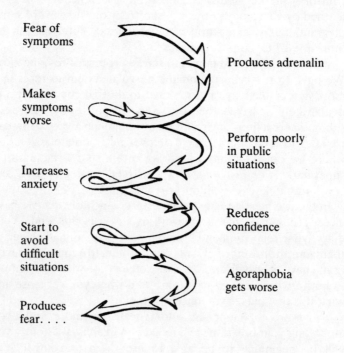

Fear of symptoms

Produces adrenalin

Makes symptoms worse

Perform poorly in public situations

Increases anxiety

Reduces confidence

Start to avoid difficult situations

Agoraphobia gets worse

Produces fear. . . .

What has been added here is the fact that the experience of symptoms makes us lose confidence, and that increases our anxiety symptoms and makes us uncomfortable so that we perform badly in public. We don't concentrate, so we seem hesitant. We may fumble our money at the till, or say silly things, or even hold on to the wall or whatever. It's all part of the downward spiral, but we can make it part of the upward spiral. How do we turn the spiral around?

Making a start

If this all seems a little complicated don't worry. What it means is that there are many things that you can do to change your life. It may have seemed that you were in a hopeless situation, trapped inside your agoraphobia. In fact your agoraphobia is a small part of your life, admittedly a part that has got out of proportion, but you have many resources which you can use to deal with it. You simply have to go about it in a matter-of-fact way and just get on with it.

The tools of the trade you have to use are everyday exercises, the keeping of a diary, small changes in your daily habits which you can use to get rid of this agoraphobia and in so doing turn your life around. There is no magic, nothing is needed apart from your own determination.

What you must do is attack that downward spiral at every point you can, using whatever methods you can. You have to take it on, study it, know it, work at it and defeat it. You have to understand your symptoms and the physical things which make them worse so that you can become less frightened by them. You have to use your relaxation and breathing techniques to reduce the impact of your symptoms, and in so doing put yourself back in charge of your body. Once you have even the slightest sense that you are making an impact your confidence will grow and that will reduce your symptoms. It will also improve your performance in public and your confidence will grow, and so on.

As you concentrate on the things we have discussed and work at them, you will begin to notice that the awful fearful feeling, the

47

sensation of dread which dominates and limits your life, will cease to be the powerful sensation it was. It may be hard to imagine what that will be like. You may have forgotten what it was like before your agoraphobia started, but as you progress the memory will stir and you will smile again. That fixed, tense expression which you need to use in public will be a thing of the past, gone and forgotten for ever. But there is a catch.

If you are someone who can't go out at all, I haven't asked you to do so until now. If you are someone who can't face certain difficult situations, I haven't suggested that you should. Alas, there will come a time soon when you will have to start facing situations which you might find difficult. Much of what I will have to say in this book from now on will be about the way you do things, the way you tackle difficult situations, how you diffuse crises and how you use your new-found skills. There is a bottom line, and that bottom line is that you will actually have to face the situations which you find difficult if you are to overcome your problems. That is common sense. Clearly you cannot solve your problems from an armchair and then suddenly get up and go out into the world cured – that would be much too easy.

The art of overcoming your agoraphobia is to make the task of dealing with your difficult situations as easy as possible, certainly easy enough for you to manage, which may be a relief to you. If you simply went out and faced your worst situation you would have little chance of dealing with it successfully, and if you didn't deal with it successfully you would simply make the problem worse.

Avoidance

Before we get down to the details, there is one more important bit of information to collect. The more knowledge you have before you start getting to grips with your problem physically, the easier overcoming it will be. What you have to look at now is avoidance behaviour, and that means working with your diary some more. If you suffer from agoraphobia, it is almost certain that you are avoiding some difficult situations. Everyone avoids some difficult situations if they are at all human – we all know our limits – but it is likely that you are avoiding some situations which other people might think are simple and non-threatening.

You might be completely housebound and be avoiding going out of the front door. You might be avoiding public transport, or going shopping, or to the cinema or theatre. Or your avoidance may be more subtle – you may only go to the supermarket with your husband so that you are avoiding going alone, or you may be avoiding looking people in the eye or you may avoid making casual conversation. You may have excellent and genuine excuses for your avoidance behaviour, but if you are avoiding any situation for any reason you should know about it and you should be honest with yourself about it.

You must know all about the situations you are avoiding – what they are, where they are and why. You may be avoiding places because of crowds, or because of the silence, or because of height, or you may be avoiding a friend's house because you have an animal phobia and they have a dog or a cat. If you have never thought about your avoidance behaviour, think now. Don't just think, start writing. Make a list of all the things you may be avoiding. Even that isn't enough. Take your diary out with you for a week and make a specific note of everything you avoid, right down to the finest detail. If you avoid sitting in the front row of a meeting when you really should, write it down. If you avoid sitting at a particular table in the canteen because you are avoiding someone whose company you find difficult, write that down.

You must have a detailed picture of your problem in its entirety, and soon you will have to stop avoiding. Doing that is part of getting back to a normal life – that is your object, and it is an object you will achieve. Like everything else we will do in this book, we will take it slowly because it would be self-defeating simply to stop avoiding difficult situations overnight even if that were possible. We must take it nice and easy, creep up on the solutions, but first we must know what our problem is, and we must know in detail. You cannot solve a problem you do not understand.

The object of all this attention to avoidance behaviour is that if you are to overcome your agoraphobia you have to stop avoiding difficult situations. It is the avoidance which is keeping your agoraphobia going, which is stoking up the agoraphobic fire. You can avoid difficult situations for much of the time, but you cannot be certain that you can *always* do so, and it is the fear of having to face a situation which is threatening and which you cannot avoid which keeps the adrenalin flowing. You have to know with absolute certainty that you can deal with any situation which you are likely to face no matter how bad you may be feeling. When you have that confidence you will have defeated your agoraphobia. You will be in charge of your life again, but you will not be able to do that unless you have dealt successfully with the problem of avoidance.

You can deal with this and all of your other problems if you go about it in the right way, and that is by a gentle, gradual approach which is itself non-threatening. I am not going to ask you to do anything which you might find too difficult simply because that would be self-defeating, you would simply produce adrenalin and make your symptoms worse. You will deal with your problems using stealth and cunning.

You might find all this diary-keeping and list-making tedious, but you must convince yourself that it is worth while. We are talking about achieving self-knowledge, of understanding something about yourself which you didn't know. You have been entwined in your agoraphobia, trapped within yourself and your personal problems for a long time, and it is time that you took an objective view and dismantled your problem, laying it open so that you can look at the workings of the mechanism. You can see what the problem is, you can see how you deal with it, where you manage it and where you have failed to manage it successfully in the past. You will have found ways of dealing with your own problems, but it may be that you have found the wrong answers. Avoiding a problem is not the answer, or at least it is only a stop-gap answer and we are looking for a cure.

Keep on noticing things about the way you manage your life. Keep on becoming more and more aware, and don't be embarrassed about the things you notice. You want to do more than just overcome your agoraphobia, you want to improve every aspect of your life, and doing that will be a side-effect of your assault on your agoraphobia. You want to be socially competent, at ease in business and social situations, able to meet people and put them at their ease, able to go to interviews and meetings and so to improve the quality of your life.

A small step

Being that confident, relaxed and successful individual may seem a long way from being the sort of person who is fearful of going out, who avoids invitations to parties and shuns social occasions, and who is never at ease in a public situation. If you are ill at ease in these situations, you may feel that you will never be the relaxed and comfortable sort of person you would like to be, and yet there is no reason why you should not be. There is a thin line which divides the relaxed from the tense, the comfortable from the uncomfortable. Remember that we are talking about one thing, the production of adrenalin from two small glands in your body. If you can control the level of adrenalin in your bloodstream, and control your breathing, you will be exactly the same as everyone else.

You can step across that dividing line, and it is a very small step to take. You have to make the right moves, you have to be organized, and most of all you have to want to do it, but if you do want to do it you can. If you are using your agoraphobia as an excuse for not succeeding at the things you want to succeed at, you will not cross that dividing line. If you really want to succeed, then nothing will stop you.

Points to remember

- Agoraphobia is a learned condition.
- Any phobia can be 'unlearned'.

- Attack your agoraphobia in any way you can.
- Discover which situations you are avoiding.
- Avoiding difficult situations makes your agoraphobia worse.

6

Dealing with the Problem

When you are out in public you might feel as if you are abroad on a shark-infested sea in a boat with a leak. It isn't a nice feeling, and it is difficult to feel confident. Everything you encounter feels alien and threatening, and all you really want to do is to get back to the safety of dry land – your home – as soon as possible.

You have now collected quite a lot of evidence about your particular problem, and this is the key to finding a solution. Everyone has a different problem, even though the fundamentals are the same, and it is your particular problem which you have to solve. Some people are completely housebound by their agoraphobia so that simply going out seems impossible. Other people might seem to have only minor difficulties in certain situations, but those difficulties might seriously limit their lives, block their promotion at work or cause them difficulties with such things as travel.

It is time to move on, to step off the curb and head off across the road. I hope you have done the necessary preparation, learned and practised relaxation exercises to the best of your ability, and that you have studied your problem with the help of a pencil and paper. I hope that you know and understand the things which make your agoraphobia worse, and the things which you may be avoiding. I hope that you now have the tools which will help you to defeat your problem. Now is the time when you will actually have to begin to face those situations which you find difficult. You have to do that carefully, taking things one step at a time so that you can achieve your objectives without too much stress. That will take thought and planning, and as there is still a long way to go, it will take time.

Going out

Difficulty going out is something which by definition everyone who suffers from agoraphobia experiences. It may be just going out of the house which is difficult, or it may be that you can do that but you can't go to a social event or shopping. You will know what your problem is.

Going out is an event for someone who suffers from agoraphobia. Most people don't give it a thought, but for you going out is difficult and you don't take your ability to go out for granted. There is always a feeling of uncertainty, sometimes of wondering if you can actually do it even though you have done it so many times before.

Going out involves three distinct stages. There is the stage of anticipation, the realization that there is somewhere you have to go, or something you have to do. That is the stage of dread, the terrible feeling that something is going to happen, that you won't be able to cope or that you will make a public exhibition of yourself. During this phase, even in the comfort and privacy of your own home, you will experience awful symptoms. The anticipation phase lasts until you leave your house.

Then there is the stage of going to the event, whether it be going to a party, going shopping, or even just going for a walk if your agoraphobia is severe. You might feel different during this stage because you are actually doing something, which might distract you from your symptoms. This stage includes the point at which you have to make contact with the people you are to be among.

Lastly, there is the stage when you are at the event and you have to maintain your public persona. This might be very difficult, especially if you are somewhere where you are conspicuous.

These three stages may occur every weekday morning if you go out to work, or they might be infrequent if you are not in the habit of going out. You have to manage each of these phases and deal with the symptoms you may experience in each case. To do that you have to use the skills you have learned and actually put them into effect, but you are hoping to achieve much more than just managing the physical problems associated with going out, you want first to control and then to rid yourself completely of the unpleasant adrenalin symptoms you experience. You want to turn that spiral the other way up and start to build your confidence. If you are to do that, you need a plan.

Making a plan

If you are working towards an objective, it helps if you know what that objective is. It is time that we defined just what it is we wish to achieve. Of course we could write down anything, but I have something specific in mind. I would like you to identify something which you would like to be able to do comfortably, something which you now find difficult but at the same time something which it is possible for you to practise, something which is within your everyday experience. It might be a visit to the supermarket by yourself. It might be a trip to the cinema or theatre, or a bus journey within the local area. It might just be a walk down the main street. It has to be something attainable, something within the bounds of possibility, something which you can't do comfortably now, and something which you would like to be able to do.

If you just went out and did this task, whatever it might be, you would experience unpleasant symptoms and it wouldn't be the enjoyable event it should be even if you had perfected the use of your relaxation and breathing exercises. How can you go about conquering this difficult situation? If you force yourself to do it your symptoms will be worse, yet if you avoid it you will never master it. What can you do?

Get out a piece of paper and write this situation down at the top of the page. At the bottom of the page write down a situation which is only very mildly threatening. It might be just standing at the front door, or it might be walking to the corner with your wife or husband, or it might be driving down the main street. It could be anything, but it should be something which makes you just a little uncomfortable, just a little ill at ease. Now fill in four or five stages in between these two extremes, events of increasing difficulty for you but events which you can practise.

This list of symptoms is called the 'situation hierarchy'. The situations on it are of increasing difficulty and form a ladder up which you can climb one step at a time. Everyone will have a different situation hierarchy according to their own particular problem, so let us take as examples two such situation ladders which are drawn up by two people with agoraphobia. When we were discussing their problems this is what they had to say.

Linda

As time has gone on I have found it more and more difficult to go out at all. The very thought of going out makes me feel ill and sometimes I just can't do it. I rely heavily on my husband, and he now does most of the shopping, though I go with him as often as I can. What I would like to be able to do is to go to the supermarket by myself and just do my shopping. I suppose my least difficult task would be going for a walk with the dog in the evening when it's quiet.

This is Linda's ladder. Start at the bottom and work up:

Shopping alone in the supermarket
Going to the supermarket at a busy time, accompanied
Going to the supermarket at a quiet time and staying a short time
Going down the main street to the post office
Going to McCrae's shop at a busy time and buying a few items
Going into McCrae's shop at a quiet time and making a purchase
Going for a walk by myself to the shopping centre
Going for a walk with the dog in the evening

Linda had drawn up a situation ladder with eight rungs, eight steps for her to climb. My other friend was a young man called John.

John

Things are getting worse. My social life is beginning to suffer and people are beginning to notice. I get so panicky at parties and I have just stopped going to discos. I can't stand the noise. I just get tearful and upset, and very shaky. I used to go to the theatre a lot, and to the cinema. I have stopped that now because when it gets quiet, even in the cinema during a tense scene, I feel terrible. I get all the symptoms including a feeling that I might shout out which is awful. I've lost all confidence. My easiest thing would be going into a bar at a quiet time, and I think my worst is a formal concert, particularly during the slow movements.

Start at the bottom rung:

Going to a classical music concert
Going to the theatre or an event on a busy night with friends
Going to a theatre or concert locally on a quiet night
Going to the cinema at a busy time, usually Saturday
Going to the cinema at a quiet time, with a friend
Going to a bar at a busy time
Going to a bar or the club in the evening

John's list of difficult situations was different from Linda's, and the opportunities he had to practise it were much harder to arrange, but it dealt with his particular problems and he just had to make the best arrangement he could.

Arranging practice

The logic of this gentle approach to the mastery of difficult situations is quite simple and well accepted. If you proceed by slow steps you will be less likely to trigger that adrenalin reaction, and by practising the easier situations first you learn to gain control of your body in that situation before you move on to the next, more difficult situation. That's all there is to it. But it won't be very easy. The theory is easy, the practice is not; so here are some tips which will help you to succeed.

Managing your symptoms

Firstly, you must understand that you will get your symptoms in public places. No one can guarantee that you will be able to go out and be symptom-free everywhere, and in any case that isn't the point of this difficult exercise. What you are seeking to do is to manage your symptoms in the situations you have chosen, to live with them, know them and know that they will do you no harm. As with avoidance behaviour, you cannot live your life dreading the onset of an adrenalin reaction because if you do that you will always be stoking up your adrenalin with the fear of the thing you are trying to avoid. It is the fear of the fear which has caused your problem, and that is what you are now going to get rid of.

When you go into your least threatening situation, you will get some symptoms. You know that. You also know that these symptoms are physiological and can do you no harm, and you know that other people will not notice them unless you say something about them or draw attention to them. So you have no need to fear your symptoms, they are simply a nuisance like indigestion or mild toothache, but the only way to convince yourself of that fact is to actually experience the symptoms in the real situation, to control them with your relaxation techniques, and to enjoy your evening or whatever and to come out of the experience at the other end feeling that you have achieved something. If you can do that you can be proud of yourself because you will have turned the corner, and you will be on the road to recovery.

You will worry that something might happen, that you might get a panic attack or fall over or faint or die. You might get a panic attack if you are prone to them, but if you do you should be pleased because it will help you to learn to manage that symptom in the real situation, and the more often you can do that the easier it will be to defeat it. Practice doesn't make perfect, but practice reduces the severity of your symptoms and makes them less frightening. After a few weeks you should be able to have a panic attack, if that is something you tend to experience, while you are talking to someone without their knowing anything is wrong. You won't even pause in your conversation, and when you have reached that stage the total conquest of your agoraphobia isn't far away.

How can you define the end point when your agoraphobia has gone? It could be the total disappearance of your symptoms, but then everyone gets some anxiety in some extreme situations. A more practical definition of the end point might be to say that it is when you can get your worst symptoms in the worst situations and not mind in the least. That is when you know that you can handle anything, and after that things will simply get better.

Putting your programme into effect

In many ways this is the most difficult thing. Just really wanting to overcome your agoraphobia doesn't necessarily mean you will automatically organize a sensible programme and put it into effect. Some people really want to lose weight, really want to get fit or really want to stop smoking, and yet they don't succeed. It takes extraordinary will power and a lot of help, as well as a few tricks of the trade. Actually adhering to your situation hierarchy is just as difficult. There is every opportunity for backsliding, for making excuses, for not having time. You have to be aware of that and minimize the possibility of such things happening.

One way to do it is to write down your practice, what you did and how long you did it. Note the severity of your symptoms and how well you managed them. Tell your husband or wife to keep you at it, and do anything you can to make sure that you practise every day.

Make sure that you have satisfactorily learned to manage one situation before you go on to the next. Don't test yourself, don't say: 'I feel OK today, I think I'll go to the supermarket.' Keep to the schedule. If you have a bad week and things don't go well, don't despair – just go back to an easier task. Much of my time is spent encouraging people to keep working on their problem, even though progress is slow and discouraging. You have to do that for yourself.

Setting the right tasks

As it is so difficult to stick to your programme, it is of vital importance that you set the right programme in the first place. There is no point in setting up tasks which you have to travel to perform, or which involve other people. Your symptom hierarchy has to be a list of situations of increasing difficulty which you can practise every day and which overall it isn't too difficult for you to achieve. If your problem is going out into your local streets, or your local shops or supermarket, then there is no great difficulty in setting up your practice.

John's symptom hierarchy would be much more difficult to organize. He could easily tackle the initial practice involving local bars and clubs, but getting to a concert regularly isn't so easy. If you are in this situation you just have to do the best you can. Frequent practice is essential, so you have to organize something you can practise frequently, so John might be better working on his ability to go into bars at busy times and to be with other people, adding his visits to concerts where and when he can.

Using relaxation exercises

If you have difficulty practising a particular situation, you can practise it in your imagination. Practising in this way is less effective than doing the real thing, but it is possible. You may have found that if you imagine a difficult situation, you can actually experience some of the unpleasant symptoms you would normally associate with that situation if you were really there. The time to do that practice is at the end of a relaxation session, after you have finished the tightening and relaxing exercises and when you are physically relaxed. If at that time you think of the situation you find difficult instead of invoking a relaxing scene, you will experience your symptoms and you will have the opportunity of using your relaxation to control them in exactly the same way as you might do in the real situation.

This would be one way forward for John. When he had got to grips with the local situations he found difficult, he could add his difficulty with concerts by using his imagination. Using relaxation sessions is also an option for someone who has severe agoraphobia and who just can't get started at all. You can always practise in your imagination, but there must come a time when you face the real situations – there is just no other way of building our confidence.

Desensitization

Constant exposure to small doses of something to which you are allergic will reduce the severity of that allergic reaction, and in medicine this is called 'desensitization'. The same term is used by psychologists for what is a very similar process. Repeated exposure to a situation which you find threatening reduces the severity of the symptoms you experience in that situation – it actually gets better.

Take as an example public speaking, something most of us find difficult. The more you rehearse, the easier your speech is and the fewer unpleasant symptoms you experience on the night. The more you speak in public the easier it is because you get used to the sensations you get when you stand up and start speaking; you know that you aren't going to break down and stutter because you never do.

For you, just going out might be like speaking in public, but if you rehearse going out over and over again, the impact of going out will decrease and you will get used to the symptoms you experience, begin to look on them as normal, and then as they decrease in importance they will decrease in severity.

There is a simple logic to all of this and it is easy to understand, just as your agoraphobia is easy to understand. There isn't any need for mumbo-jumbo. You don't need to resort to hypnosis or to any other form of treatment. All you need is your common sense and your determination. You need to be systematic and you mustn't try to take short cuts. If you do the exercise and if you stick to the rules you will make rapid progress at first. As time goes on your progress will slow down a bit and you might even feel that you aren't getting anywhere, but if you keep at it you will continue to progress slowly and steadily. You will notice that you want to do more with your life, and that you are able to do more.

Points to remember

- Practising difficult situations makes them easier to manage.
- Arrange to practise as often as you can.
- Practise easier situations first.
- Progress in easy stages.
- With practice your symptoms will be less intrusive.
- With practice your confidence will return.

7

Some more Tricks of
the Trade

So far there has been a lot of hard work. Doing relaxation and breathing exercises, keeping your diary, working out your situation hierarchy, it is all very much like going back to school, yet overcoming your agoraphobia is a learning exercise so perhaps you do have to go back to school. Still, school should be fun, and overcoming agoraphobia should be an enjoyable and rewarding experience.

The reward comes in finding that you can actually do more than you thought you could, that you can go to parties and survive, and perhaps even enjoy yourself. One of the most distressing things about agoraphobia is that it removes the enjoyment from almost everything you try to do. The feeling of apprehension, the wondering 'Should I, shouldn't I go?' which precedes every event, the downright discomfort before and during the event, the wanting to leave before the event finishes, all this is miserable and you deserve better.

You may have felt that that is all that life has to offer you, but you were wrong. Life can be rich and rewarding for everyone, and it can be for you. You really must believe that, and you must reach out for that kind of happiness and achievement no matter what age you are, no matter what situation you are in. You have to have that kind of confidence, and confidence is what life is all about. One of the things which has contributed to the development of your agoraphobia has been your loss of confidence. You may have confidence overall, knowing that you are as good as the next man or the next woman, but when it comes to putting that confidence into practice it all comes apart.

Lack of confidence leads to a poor performance in public so that you don't do yourself justice, and at the end of an evening you come home dispirited. Another contributor to your problem may be that you have an easily aroused automatic nervous system, so that you automatically turn on the adrenalin sooner than others might, and so develop adrenalin symptoms earlier than most. This is a physical problem, but the development of symptoms in public leads to that poor performance and so to a lack of confidence. Let's look at the downward spiral again. How else can we twist its tail and turn it into an upward spiral?

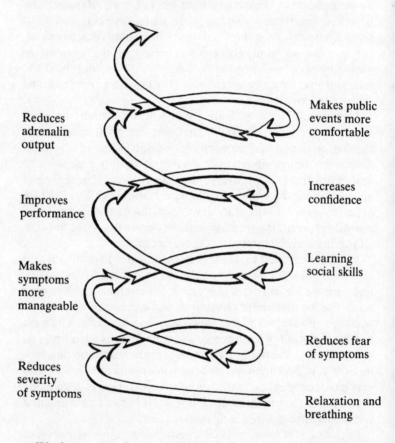

Reduces adrenalin output

Makes public events more comfortable

Improves performance

Increases confidence

Makes symptoms more manageable

Learning social skills

Reduces severity of symptoms

Reduces fear of symptoms

Relaxation and breathing

We have seen how relaxation and breathing exercises can reduce the severity of our symptoms, and how repetition and practice can make our symptoms less severe in certain situations, but is there anywhere else where we can attack our agoraphobic spiral? One other possible way of intervening in this system is in the area of public performance.

Public performance

Most of us think of a public performance as some kind of acting, of appearing like actors on a stage, but that isn't what I mean by public performance in this context. I mean that what we do in public, the way we move and the way we talk, the way we do things, all of these are in some way a performance, or rather a presentation of ourselves for the benefit of others. No one is completely natural in public, totally unselfconscious, and that is just as well. We modify our behaviour for others, we change what we say and the way we say it, and in that way communication and relationships are possible. If we were all totally honest and never told even a white lie we would have no wife or husband, no friends and probably no job. Life is a constant matter of adjustment and performance.

There is a school of psychology which believes that all of life is a performance, that we are all just acting out a role. Most of us, however, would like to believe that there are times, those private and personal times, when we are ourselves. The implication is not that we are false in public, not that we are trying to deceive, but that in order to communicate, relate and survive we have to have a public face. That public persona develops over the years and is as much a part of us as anything else – and this may well be part of the problem.

We have seen that some of the problems of agoraphobia such as the symptoms, the breathing habits and the tensions, are learned. We have developed symptoms, avoided difficult situations and our agoraphobia has grown. Now we are talking about learning to project a public persona over the years, and you might conclude, correctly, that you may have learned the wrong lessons. Once things have started to go wrong, you can develop an inappropriate or inadequate public face and that can cause problems. As with other things, if you perform badly in public, if you know that you are clumsy, if you say the wrong things and as a result don't do yourself justice when you are with others, you will lose confidence and spin the spiral faster. As with other things, you can do something about it. You can improve your public performance and that is something you should consider.

Improving your performance

Just practising and rehearsing the situations you find difficult will help to improve your performance, but you need to do more than just practise a difficult situation. You will need to identify those parts of your performance which you do badly and you need to develop techniques which will help you to improve those specific parts. Performance is important because the way you present yourself is the way other people see you, and if you know that they see you as a nervous clumsy person in public then that is the way you will feel. If you believed that other people saw you as a relaxed, comfortable, debonair person, then it would be easier for you to appear in public places. It is just another trick, another way of turning that spiral the other way up so that you can start to feel more comfortable and more relaxed in public.

You have to polish up your performance and try to project a more relaxed image. If you are to do that you need to learn special techniques, and you need to do some work. By now that is nothing less than you would expect, but think of the benefits! If you *know* that you can appear relaxed even though you are feeling terrible, if you know that other people were wishing that they were as relaxed as you are even though you are feeling awful, how much easier it would be for you to manage that situation. At the moment a great deal of your time and effort goes into worrying about how you seem to others to be coping, and whether they will notice that something is wrong. You have to know that you can project the right image no matter what.

You have to get it right. Where do you start? Well, you have already started. What about your relaxation exercises? If you can master them at home you can use them in public – anywhere, anytime. You don't have to go through the muscle squeezing and relaxing, you just have to evoke that feeling of relaxation, and if you make a habit of doing that it will soon come naturally. You have to relax deliberately, you have to sit in a relaxed way. You have to breathe slowly and let your muscles go loose. Use the time after a relaxation session to practise, but bear in mind that, like everything else about overcoming agoraphobia, it takes time and work, it takes effort just to be the same as other people (but then, of course, you don't know how much effort they are putting into being the same as other people).

If just sitting in a corner looking relaxed was all you ever had to do practising relaxation would be enough, but you have to do more than that. You have to use public transport, go into shops, go to interviews, stand in crowds, all stressful events for you. You have to manage the rising symptoms of panic and know that other people won't notice. You have to be able to sit in a cinema or a seat at the local children's concert feeling that you are going to choke or cry, and yet be absolutely sure that you will appear normal.

Think of the great security that knowledge would give you, and how it would improve your confidence, and yes, that would reduce the severity of your symptoms and things would get better. How can you achieve that blissful state where you appear to be in control, even if you don't feel as if you are? Well, there are no special tricks, just the well-tried methods we have used before.

Your diary again

It should be no surprise if we return to your diary for help. Much of the thrust of what we have been attempting to do has been to raise to a conscious level things which others usually take for granted. Most people give a natural uninhibited performance, while someone who suffers from agoraphobia struggles and doesn't really know why. Now is the time to make a few notes about your performance.

Make your notes, as before, at the time things happen. It

might be notes about the way you walk down the street. Do you walk in a natural way? Who or what do you look at? Do you walk too fast or too slow, and do you stand up straight or are you stooped and apologetic? These aren't trivial matters, they are the bricks and mortar out of which your image is formed. What about the way you speak to people? What do you say and how do you say it? How do you manage in shops? What does your voice sound like? Is it natural, or is it forced or strained? You have plenty of scope for using your pencil and paper to record the areas where you have difficulty. Recording them may help you to define areas where you can improve your performance, and the act of writing things down may by itself help you to be aware and to improve things without your really knowing that you are doing so. But you can do more than that. You can work to improve on your performance in a positive and constructive way.

I was talking to a young man whose name was Simon. He had been keeping a diary for some time, and I asked him to keep a record of some of the situations he had to face where his performance was not as he would have liked it to be. When he came back to see me, this is what he had to say.

Simon

Well, I never do myself justice. I always feel that I'm making a fool of myself, but it's just the symptoms that I get really. How can you seem relaxed and comfortable when you have a tremor, or if you feel as if you are going to get diarrhoea? How can you talk to girls if you are feeling dizzy?

The first problem I get is in the morning when I'm waiting for the bus. I just feel sick, so that when the bus comes I have difficulty getting the right fare. When I get to my seat I feel as if everyone is looking at me and I get very anxious and uncomfortable. I always feel that I might have to get off to go to the toilet, though I never have yet. I had a meeting on Tuesday. I should have given a report, but I couldn't. I just said that everything was all right, even though I knew I should have asked a few pertinent questions.

The worst thing of the week was the party on Friday night. I had a terrible time before I went out, but the real problem was just going in through the door. I met people but I really can't remember much about it. I don't know what to say to people, particularly girls, and when I do say something it sounds stupid. I'm much too involved in the way I feel. In the end I just came home by myself early, and it was a relief to get away.

Church as usual was a nightmare. I can't stand the silence. When we do sing hymns I have to mime because my throat closes up and I can't sing. During the prayers I think I am going to die, I just can't breathe.

Here was a young man who seems to be leading a very full life. He could go to work, travel on a bus, go to meetings and even go to parties. On Sundays he would go to church, so he didn't seem to be avoiding difficult situations. He had already made considerable progress, but he was still getting symptoms, still lacking in confidence, and he was getting dispirited. He had to do more.

Rehearsal and practice

Over the years that Simon had been agoraphobic he had forgotten some of the skills that most people take for granted, so that when he started to do the things he had previously not been doing, what was missing was the ability to communicate with and relate to others. His difficulty in doing this undermined his confidence and that created problems of its own. What he would have to do now was to start to learn the 'social skills' he had either forgotten or perhaps never mastered.

These social skills are many and varied, and cover everything from the ability to make a speech to how much you should meet someone's eye when you are talking to them. Every detail is important, and every detail can be improved by rehearsal and practice. First you have to identify the things which you find difficult, and which may be holding you back in your everyday life, and then you have to do something about it. You can only appear confident and relaxed by hard work and effort.

How do you manage a conversation? How do you know how

well you manage a conversation? It would be nice if you had a video camera covering every aspect of your daily life, but you haven't. What you can do is to stand back from yourself, try to see your entry to the party or whatever it might be, as if you were an observer, or a video camera. It is possible to form some sort of objective impression of just how well you perform.

How about conversations? If you have never had a conversation with yourself in the mirror it's time you had. You can watch yourself in a mirror, and you can listen to yourself on a cassette player, though not necessarily at the same time. What do you look like when you are relaxed, and when you are talking? Do you look relaxed and confident, and if you don't, what can you change to achieve that effect? How often do you meet the other person's eyes? If you do it too much you appear aggressive and make them uncomfortable; too little and you seem uninterested. You get it right by practice.

Do you laugh too much? Do you talk too much? How do you manage silences? This last one can be very difficult. There is always a temptation to jump in with an inane comment when conversation lags and there is a silence, but a person who has the confidence to remain silent gives the impression of being totally relaxed and at ease. There is the 'art of conversation', and this is an art form you can learn and improve, and if you are comfortable in conversation, your confidence will grow. Practise looking at yourself, and listening to yourself.

What we are talking about is the image of yourself which you project, and if that image is right, you can be more relaxed. It has to be an image of you, it can't be false or you couldn't sustain it, but it has to do you justice. If you think that others see you as a bumbling fool, then you will cringe in public. If you know that no matter how ill at ease you may be feeling you will look relaxed and comfortable, then it will be much easier for you to stay where you are and ride out the storm of your symptoms. If you can do that, and continue to do that, then your symptoms will decrease.

What do you say?

It might be possible to think of agoraphobia as a condition in which one gets unpleasant symptoms in great empty spaces, or in anonymous crowds, but where there are people there is communication, and so you have to learn how you can best achieve the best and most relaxed conversation and communication. If you find this difficult when you are flustered, learn a few conversational gambits, learn what you can say comfortably, and know that you can make the necessary conversational moves even though you are stressed. What do you say to the bus driver when you have to pay your fare, or to the shop assistant, or to the bank clerk? The little pieces of social chat which others seem to make so easily aren't so easy, and you may have to invent your own and learn them.

It's all to do with going on autopilot. When things are bad and you are sweating, you are feeling panicky and your throat is tight, you will be more at ease if you can smile and say 'Good morning. Nice day, isn't it?' without any thought. You need to practise party talk, business talk, travel talk, gambits for any occasion.

This is what Simon, the person we met earlier, had to do. He had to learn how to manage certain specific situations: the bus journey, meetings, parties and church. He had already worked on a situation hierarchy and was out and about, but he still had problems with symptoms and with confidence, and if he was to keep managing his daily life he had to identify these problems and learn how to deal with them.

Work at it

If you have done your exercises, if you have drawn up a situation hierarchy and have managed to break the grip of your agoraphobia enough to let you start to live your life, what you now need is more confidence, and in the field of confidence building, nothing succeeds like success. You can help yourself to deal successfully with difficult situations by practising them and perfecting your social skills in private, so that managing conversations and events such as Simon's meeting becomes habit, so that you can do the talking and use the correct mannerisms without conscious effort.

Simon had to have the 'patter' to deal with the bus driver, and he had to learn the art of sitting quietly in a relaxed way as he had to do on the bus and in church, so that in those situations he would know that he looked relaxed and that other people would take him as being relaxed and confident. Some people do these things automatically, some have to work at them. If you suffer from agoraphobia, you have to work at them, practise them and rehearse them until you get to the point where, if an emergency happens, you can rely on your practice and training to see you through.

Confidence is built on hard work. Make time to do it. Use your diary to plan it and make sure that you do practise the things you find difficult, and, most of all, really work at it.

Points to remember

- Practising difficult situations makes them easier to manage.
- You can learn social skills.
- You have to be able to manage situations you find difficult without having to think about them.
- Learning a few conversational gambits makes social situations easier.
- Successfully managing social situations increases your confidence.

8

Getting Out and About

So far we have used relaxation and similar techniques to release you from the chains of your agoraphobia, so that you should by now be able to do much more than before. By working your way painstakingly up your situation hierarchy you should have achieved competence in an area of your choice, but you have also had to understand that being able to do things isn't exactly the same as enjoying doing them or feeling relaxed while doing them.

Constantly going out and doing things does make the exercise less stressful and reduces the severity of your symptoms, and learning new skills and improving old ones makes for greater confidence which also reduces the severity of symptoms, so if you are following the advice in this book you are travelling down the right road, albeit a hard and rocky road. When your symptoms subside and your confidence grows you are home and dry.

It all sounds very easy, and in theory it is. In practice, as you will know very well, it is very difficult and you need all the help you can get. It just isn't easy to go out and face a hostile world, and there will be times when some situations seem to be impossible to manage. There will be failures and disappointments, but your successes will far outweigh your failures. Every time you do something which you thought you might never be able to do again is an achievement. Often these successes are small, but don't underestimate them because you build on your successes, and every time you have any sort of achievement, the next step will be easier.

The hostile world

The world seems hostile because you experience your symptoms when you venture into it, and you do that because your body perceives the world to be dangerous. You will know that the world seems less hostile if you are accompanied by somebody, even if that somebody is a child who has no understanding of your problems. You need a friend to relate to, so that you are not a stranger in a foreign land. You might be able to arrange to be accompanied by a friend on many occasions, but of course the point of overcoming your agoraphobia is so that you can go places by yourself. You may have been dependent on other people for years, and now you want to be independent.

The experience of loneliness when you are agoraphobic and in a threatening place is a powerful and all-pervading one. Total collapse and breakdown seem just round the corner, and that thought is terrifying. The fact that collapse doesn't come and that your symptoms lead to nothing doesn't help, you still feel terrible. All that has been said before should make it easier for you, but you must have the determination to keep at it in spite of the way you feel. Let's see what else you can do that will help you tackle difficult situations.

Planning

When you are faced with a new situation, which might happen if you are proceeding up your situation ladder or if an unexpected event such as a wedding occurs, you can be gripped by uncertainty or even panic. Will you be able to cope? How will you manage?

All that has been said previously is relevant, but to that repertoire of skills you can add *planning*. Anticipation and fear of the unknown can be worse than the event itself, so that the more you know about an event you are going to attend the better. You will need to know exactly what will be expected of you, where the event will be, when you will be expected to arrive and when you will be able to leave. If the event is an important one like a wedding, it would be worth while going to the hotel in advance. Just drop in for a drink and give the place the once over, just so that when you arrive on the day it won't be a completely new experience.

Make it your business to find out as much about the event as possible, and plan your participation in it as best you can. Don't be too rigid, because then if you are forced to do something you hadn't planned for you may feel panicky.

Do as much as possible of the organization of your own part in the event beforehand. Ask the right questions. Who will be there? How long will it last? Sort out how you are going to get home so that you aren't dependent on other people and you can leave in your own time. Remember that you aren't trying to avoid difficult situations, and that you have to be ready for the unexpected, but make sure that you have a head start over everyone else. The more you know about the event the better you can practise and rehearse, for example by thinking up a few conversation pieces which might help you.

Going out to an event

We have already mentioned the three stages of any event. The first, and perhaps the worst, is the anticipation. Then there is going to the event. And then there is being there and staying there, getting through to the end. All three are tough.

Anticipation

The phase of anticipation can start days before, or it might be worse on waking on the morning of the event, or it might be bad just before you go out. In every case it can be much worse than the event itself. You will experience the full adrenalin reaction, you may pace the floor and wring your hands in anguish, have diarrhoea repeatedly, feel dizzy or sick, and all for a school concert or a social evening. How do you deal with that? You experience it every time despite your relaxation and breathing exercises. The problem is that your symptoms are so powerful that you reach the threshold of control every time, so that the repeated experience of the symptoms merely reinforces what is happening and you do not become desensitized.

You have to go through the anticipation phase and keep doing it until you burn it out, by finding ways of reducing the trauma to manageable proportions. The first thing is to resolve that you are actually going to go out so that there is no equivocation, no 'Will I, won't I?'. Decide right at the start whether you are going to go or not, so that all you have to do is to find a way of managing this period.

The first thing *not* to do is to walk up and down. Any kind of physical exercise gets your adrenalin going and makes things worse. Try to sit quietly in that period up to your departure from the house. Imagine that someone is looking at you and try to project an image of quiet relaxation. Look relaxed, feel relaxed. Let the physical tension in your muscles flow out. Make sure that you have made the arrangements for your departure in advance so that you don't have to fumble for keys or hunt for a raincoat. You don't need any hassle.

You may have problems with diarrhoea, or rather with intestinal hurry, which isn't quite the same thing. Your intestine may go into overdrive and you may feel that you have to go back into the toilet. The more you go back the more you have to go back, so what do you do? You simply avoid going repeatedly to the toilet. When you feel you need to go, leave it for a few minutes. Don't rush straight back. You will find that you really can leave it without disastrous results, and if you keep delaying your return to the toilet the problem will decrease so that you will be able to leave the house without any anxiety on that score.

If there is one piece of over-riding advice which I can offer it is to *slow down*. If you are anxious, which you are if you are agoraphobic and you are having to go out, you have a tendency to speed up, to do things faster and faster. You can counter that by physically slowing down your movements.

In any difficult situation the same advice applies. Slow down your movements, slow down your speech, relax and let things happen. If you have someone with you whom you can trust, engage their help to get you relaxed and slowed down.

Going out

Eventually the time comes when you have to go out. You might expect that to be the worst time, but often it is a relief to get going. When you are actually in the car you may start to feel better, perhaps because you feel somehow purposeful. It takes courage to make the break with your home, and no one should underestimate the courage shown daily by people with agoraphobia, or any other psychological condition for that matter.

However, you are now out and you are on your way, and as you get close to your destination, you will begin to feel uneasy, and as you actually approach the door your symptoms may flood back.

Now is the time when your preparation will help. You must expect to feel flustered and uncomfortable, but if you are prepared for that and if you have rehearsed your entrance in your mind and you know whom you will meet and what you will say, you will find the situation much easier. Your heart may be racing and you may feel dizzy but you know that you can do it, and every time you do it it will be less traumatic. That is the way forward for you and for everyone who suffers from agoraphobia. You can manage the situation using the special techniques you have learned, repeating the situation as often as you can, and the situation will decrease in significance and be easier to cope with.

Being there

Once you have arrived somewhere and survived, you have to stay. That might be easy, and it often is because all that has gone before is more difficult, but there are problems with just being at a public event, too. If you are going to have to do something which will make you conspicuous then that is a problem, but even if you are a spectator or a member of the audience, there are possible trouble spots. If you know what these are you will anticipate them and worry about them. Even though you may rehearse them in your own mind at home, they can still be difficult to manage.

You may find that you keep swallowing, or that you can't get a breath, or, perhaps worst of all, that you feel tearful, as if you are going to break down and make a public exhibition of yourself. You might have a panic attack or feel dizzy, and just reading the list of symptoms may make you feel very uncomfortable. You can make a conscious appreciation of these sensations and say to yourself that they will not do you any harm. You won't break down in public. How do you know? Because you never have, and as well as that you know that many people have exactly the same problems as you have and you don't see people breaking down in public all the time, do you? There is a strong urge to conform, and that is what you will do, no matter how badly you feel.

Try not to avoid things. If you aren't comfortable in the cinema or theatre then of course you can sit at the end of the row near the exit, but if you do that you must understand that it is a form of avoidance, and if you book seats which prove to be in the middle of a row it shouldn't be a disaster. If you depend on having seats at the end of a row, you will always fear a situation where you may have to sit in the middle and you will never be comfortable going out to that sort of event. So if you go to the cinema at a quiet time, try to sit in the middle of a row and so deliberately practise doing something you find difficult. That is something you should always be trying to do.

Losing control

What happens if you are at a public event, feeling quite OK, and suddenly feel that you are starting to 'lose control'? You become aware that you are beginning to get some of your symptoms and you lose confidence. It's like swimming into the deep end when you aren't quite sure if you're an adequate swimmer or not. You are fine so long as you are close to the edge and you are relaxed, but as soon as the thought that you might sink enters your mind your pulse speeds up and you start to panic. If you are adrift at a public event the same thing can happen, and you can begin to believe that you are sinking. What do you do?

The best thing to do is to work through a checklist of possible explanations. Start with the physical possibilities first. Remember that your body may interpret physical discomfort as psychological panic, so ask yourself whether that prickly feeling down your back is due to the fact that you are starting to sweat, whether you feel dizzy because your stomach is upset and you are feeling just a bit sick. It might just be that the place is too noisy, or that you are hungry. Work through the possibilities and you will find that the instant you identify the cause of your discomfort and can give it a physical explanation you will feel better. Dealing with physical problems is easy.

If you continue to feel 'uptight', don't try to push it away and force it not to happen, because you can't. If you think that you might have a panic attack, so what? A panic attack can do you no harm so you just have to manage the situation, and now is the time to use all of the things you have practised at home. Note that it's too late now to try to use things you haven't practised as you haven't a hope of making them work for you. You have to be able to use them automatically, so just sit tight and slow your breathing, relax and let your shoulders come down. Identify the symptoms which you are experiencing so that you know what you are dealing with, and then let things happen.

Leaving

Leaving an event before it finishes is avoiding an event, so try not to do so. Every time you leave an event before you're supposed to you have suffered a small defeat, and managing that situation the next time will be more difficult. If you can stay a little longer than you thought you could, you have won a small victory and you will feel great, and the next time will be easier. It's as simple as that, but if you feel you would be happier leaving an event, do so quietly without elaborate explanations. People leave the room at parties and all sorts of events for all sorts of reasons and no one takes any notice, so why should anyone notice what you are doing? Try to stay where you are for a few moments longer than you want to and you might find that the crisis passes. Anxiety symptoms tend to peak and then fade away, so if you can manage over the peak you might find that you are able to stay after all.

If you go to a difficult event and stay, if you achieve any small victory, you have every right to congratulate yourself. What you have achieved is no mean feat and anyone who has not suffered from agoraphobia can never understand just what an effort you have made and what great courage you have shown. The important thing is that *you* know, and you can be tremendously pleased with yourself. You can look forward to the next time, and before that you can work on the things that you found difficult on this occasion. For the average person going to a party may be just going to a party, while for you it is a major expedition, something requiring planning and preparation. If you manage that situation adequately you have won a battle and you are on the way to winning the war, and that must be a source of quiet satisfaction.

Points to remember

- Anticipating an event is often worse than the event itself.
- Remember to slow down.
- Prepare for any event you have to attend as well as you can.
- Try to find physical reasons for the way you feel.
- Don't leave an event unless you have to.

9

Moving On

Overcoming your agoraphobia takes a great deal of effort and it isn't easy. The pay-off comes in the satisfaction you get in just being able to do the things which you have previously not been able to do. It comes in the return to normality, in the ability to present yourself in public places as your real self, not as some sort of mumbling apology for yourself. It is in acquiring confidence, and eventually in enjoying going to different places, seeing different things and having different experiences. It is this last subject which we need to consider now.

Getting enjoyment back into your life

Agoraphobia is a ball and chain which holds you back. It makes the most simple things in life difficult, and though with effort and practice you can do just about anything you want to do, the last thing to come back is your enjoyment of life. Doing new things is an effort, and it would be foolish to deny that. You have as much right to enjoy life as anyone else, so how can you inject that enjoyment factor back into the things that you do?

The easy answer is that you have to keep going on in the absolute belief that your life will become enjoyable as the unpleasant symptoms you experience diminish. That is a fact and you can accept that it will happen, but there is more to be done to capture that elusive happiness which is your right. Once you have achieved your immediate goals and become competent in the areas of your daily life which have been causing you trouble, you have to raise your sights and look for other targets. It isn't good enough to continue with the things you have achieved and then sit back and wait for things to progress, you have to take life by the throat and make things happen.

Here you may find a dilemma. What sort of things do you *want* to make happen? In what sort of way do you *want* to change your life? Do you have any unfulfilled ambitions? Are there things which you have wanted to do but which you have not been able to do because of your agoraphobia? It may be that you are totally satisfied with your life, but that shouldn't stop you from asking these questions. One of your problems in finding answers may be that although agoraphobia was your main and over-riding problem, it is only part of a more general problem.

Right at the beginning of this book I pointed out that people who suffer from agoraphobia tend to have high anxiety levels anyway. This may well be part of the reason why the agoraphobia developed. You may have a higher level of circulating adrenalin, and this adrenalin may be released more easily than in other people, so that your threshold of release is lower. In a situation which other people might find annoying or slightly stressful, you get a blast of adrenalin and all the associated symptoms. These situations are outside the home, and so just being outside the home may become a stressful situation.

Other phobias

Before looking at ways of extending your life it is worth checking on any other impediments which there might be. One of these might be the presence of other phobias. It is worth asking if your inability to go out to public places is entirely due to your agoraphobia, or whether there is something else which bothers you. Do you have a dog phobia which makes you worry about the possibility of having to meet and deal with a dog, or do you have a social phobia and simply have difficulty meeting people, speaking to them and knowing what to say and how to say it? It might be this type of problem which is holding you back.

Then there are difficulties with particular situations. We met someone earlier in this book who had problems with a meeting at work. He did attend the meeting, but he had problems when he was there, and after it was over he knew that he hadn't done himself justice. It could be that this particular problem was stopping him from getting promotion at work and interfering with his whole career. The problem isn't just with the meeting itself, it lies in the knowledge that from time to time there will be meetings, and the fear of the symptoms which would be experienced makes all of work unpleasant and troublesome.

Then there are other more subtle problems. If someone has a problem with parties, for example, is it just the physical circumstances of the party which are the cause of the problem? Is it the noise, the small enclosed space which we might expect to be the cause of the difficulty, or is there an added problem in the form of a worry about the possibility of having to make contact with the opposite sex? You might have a sexual hang-up, or perhaps we could call it excessive shyness. You have to be honest with yourself, and you have to be prepared to investigate the possibilities. And how do you do that?

We go back again to your diary. You should continue to keep a diary from time to time so that you can pick up problems. If you have to go to meetings and you find that difficult, why is it difficult? You may have a phobia about speaking in public, which isn't necessarily the same thing as phobia about public speaking. You might have problems marshalling your thoughts so that you can give a report, and you may not be systematic enough to collect the data you need. You have to identify your problem and then think of a practical way of dealing with it. Would it help if you made notes, or would it help if you practised in front of a mirror or with a tape-recorder? You could use relaxation exercises to rehearse the entire meeting every time you have to go to one. Find practical ways of sorting out your problems.

What about difficulties with talking to people, particularly members of the opposite sex? Again it is a matter of practice, and particularly of practice at a lower level of threat than the one which gives you problems. By that I mean that you should seek out the company of members of the opposite sex in everyday situations. At a party there is always the possibility of a sexual liaison, and for many shy people that is threatening. You should try to meet men or women at a club or in some situation where the priority isn't making a date or whatever. You should progress to the situation where boys meet girls and vice versa with a view to forming a relationship only when you feel comfortable doing so.

Your agoraphobia traps you in a tangled web. It isn't as simple as it appears at first, and you have to untangle all the strands if you are to break free and escape.

Fulfilling your ambitions

Now that you are starting to do more, you should pause for a moment and think about what you have achieved, and more importantly, what you *can* achieve. You have to do more, you owe it to yourself, and the more you achieve the easier it becomes for you to do the simple things. If you can walk into a meeting and make a speech, and you know that you can do that, then that will give you the confidence to be able to go into a local bar with a few friends and buy a round of drinks. The importance of such routine events diminishes. If you are an important person in some way, either as an office-bearer in a society or at work, then your self-esteem rises and so does your confidence. For that reason it is important that you have ambitions, and that you fulfil those ambitions.

What we are talking about here is making changes in our lives, in our lifestyle, even arguably in the sort of person we are. Who hasn't said, 'What couldn't I do if it weren't for this dreadful agoraphobia!' Now you have a challenge. If you have overcome your agoraphobia, what are you going to do? You can't be content with the same limited existence you had before, and you have the opportunity to expand your life and move on in a new direction, and that is quite a challenge, and quite a worry.

What do you want to achieve?

The first step in achieving anything is to decide exactly what it is you want to achieve, and after that you can work out how you are going to do it. If you want to change your life in any way, no matter how small, do it slowly and carefully, taking one step at a time. That might ring a bell. You will remember our situation hierarchy with the small steps you had to take then, and you can progress with any changes you wish to make in your life in exactly the same way.

Have a look at your life. See what is satisfactory and what is unsatisfactory, and see if your agoraphobia is getting in the way of the things you want to achieve. It will be easier if you do this with a pencil and paper, and at the end of the exercise make a note of what your life could be like if you removed the impediments you now have. Of course, you must make your ambitions realistic, and remember that you can't change your personality. You will always be the same you, though you can expect to be a more confident and able you.

Now write down the steps which you might take to bring you eventually to your chosen goal, and when you have a reasonable plan worked out, including some sort of timetable, you can start making the changes you want. It might help you to plan changes in your life if you try to decide what sort of person you are. We can never see ourselves in a completely objective way, but most of us have some idea of our strengths and weaknesses, and making a few notes about ourselves may help to make our plans more realistic.

A young woman called Julie worked through most of the exercises in this book and came back to see what else she could do. She had reached something of an impasse. She had been severely agoraphobic, with her activities limited to going out shopping with her husband. By her own determination, and with careful planning, she had managed to get out and about, often by herself. She had initially been very excited by her progress, but now things had slowed down and she didn't seem to be getting anywhere. What had happened was that she had achieved most of what she initially wished to achieve. She could go out by herself, and although things were still bad on occasions, she could cope with every situation. So why was she now feeling dissatisfied? The answer was that the time had come for her to do more. I asked her to go through the exercises I have just described and to come back and tell me her conclusions.

Julie

My agoraphobia was very bad when I started to work on it. Some days weren't so bad and I could do my shopping, but on bad days I just sat in the house and was miserable. That doesn't happen now. I can always go out, even though some days are still pretty rough. I can cope. I can stay on in the queue and I can even go on the bus to the city with my friends. I've just got things together and life is much easier, but I'm still not as happy as I should be.

What I would like to do is to go to the aerobics class. I thought that I might never get into a leotard, but I would like to do it now and I think I could. I know three girls who are going back to school as mature students to do computer studies and I would like to do that, though I don't know whether I could cope or not. Of course, in the long run I want to go back to work, and if I had a few more skills I could work as a secretary or receptionist again. I never thought that I would be able to do that.

Julie was lucky in that she could identify definite goals, and she knew where she was going. She could also identify some steps in between where she could get practice meeting people and being with them. Her life had been limited by her agoraphobia for so long that when she started to make progress she was clearly not going to be satisfied with a life which was based on visits to the supermarket and local shopping.

Julie wanted to enrich her life, to do more, to try more things. Once she had started to overcome her agoraphobia she was off and running, and you can be sure that when she was able to go to an aerobics class, or to go to night school or back to secondary school to catch up on her education, she wouldn't spare a thought for the problems of shopping in the supermarket. If you want to be comfortable with yourself you have to fulfil your ambitions, whatever they may be.

Finding opportunities

How can you go about enriching your life if you aren't sure which way to go? Not everyone is bursting to get into the mainstream of life, and many people have considerable apprehension regarding the future. It isn't easy to change your life, and if you have lived with agoraphobia for many years you may have developed a love–hate relationship with it. You may hate it, but at least you are familiar with it and you have learned to live with it. Now you are being told that if you are to be contented you have to sail abroad on uncertain waters and do things you aren't sure you will be able to do. It may seem unfair. What sort of things might you do?

That depends upon your interests. It depends upon your age and your experience and your personal situation, but everyone has some unfulfilled ambition or some interest he or she might want to pursue. It could be anything from sport to history or simply shopping. Many of the things you might want to do involve travelling, so that is a skill you might want to master as soon as possible. If you want to get on, do it in the way I have suggested – systematically and carefully, not missing out any steps along the way.

In short, you have to make out another situation ladder to go on top of the one you have already used, so that you can climb higher. That doesn't imply that you will become more insecure: if you have taken care to lay good, secure foundations your ladder will be quite safe, the higher you climb the easier the basic tasks all become.

Special situations

Everyone who suffers from agoraphobia comes up against special situations which can't be fitted into any situation hierarchy. You can plan them and prepare for them, but they are 'one-off' situations which just have to be faced. They include weddings, funerals, family reunions, your children's concerts and prize-givings, sports fixtures, presentations at work and a host of other things.

In these situations you have a choice: you either go or you don't go. Of course you want to go, or you feel that you have an obligation to go, and some people may assume that people who suffer from agoraphobia don't do things because they don't want to. As you will know, there is nothing that people who suffer from agoraphobia would rather do than to go to any event they want to go to without giving it a thought. Unfortunately, the agoraphobia tends to get in the way.

Of course, if you work at your agoraphobia you will be able to face most situations with confidence, but that time may be some distance away and there may always be some rarely faced situations which make you uncomfortable. Some of these events are particularly difficult because of their emotional content. A wedding can bring tears to the eyes of the most stalwart mother, funerals can be sad, and watching your child perform in public can be particularly nerve-racking. How do you manage these special situations?

There are no general rules for managing any situation, but you have learned more than a few basic principals which will help you. There's no reason why you shouldn't put them into effect in any situation you may find yourself in, and there is no reason why you should decline to attend any event you want to attend. The first step is to say 'yes' when you are asked. Don't prevaricate or hedge, or look shifty, just say a definite 'yes'. The details can look after themselves later. Once you are committed to going you just have to get on with it, and that might be a stimulus to putting into effect the exercises and techniques outlined in this book.

One thing can be added. You know that you can manage difficult situations, and you know that the situation you are approaching will be difficult. But it is going to be difficult for everyone. That is the essence of these major family or public situations, they are emotional events which are hard on everyone. Everyone attending feels the strain, and others may feel on this occasion the way you used to feel just walking down the street. The difference on this occasion is that you are used to dealing with the way you feel, and they may not be. You know how to control your body, they don't.

It would be wrong to put the emphasis on control, however. In a situation of real emotion you should be able to let yourself go and not to worry if your emotions show for once. You have to be able to let yourself go sometimes, and that is a skill you might have to learn; as always, you learn it by practice and rehearsal in private.

Agoraphobia and younger people

Younger people find themselves in a special situation because on the whole they have, and they need, a more active social life than older people. They are on the move, needing to make friends and form relationships. They need to be out and about much of the time, and so for them agoraphobia can be a particular disaster. Young people also tend to be more self-conscious than older people, and less likely to hazard themselves in situations where there might be a chance of their making a fool of themselves, or thinking that such a thing might happen.

There is no special advice for young people, there are no different techniques; they just have to have the confidence to do the exercises which other people must do. The fact that young people are so gregarious can be a help or a hindrance. If you, as a young person, have the benefit of friends who understand your problem and are prepared to give you support and help, that can be of the utmost benefit, so be prepared to seek such help. In the last chapter we will consider ways of going about getting advice and help.

Points to remember

- Be prepared to widen your horizons.
- Set yourself new goals.
- Basic tasks become easier when you are achieving more.
- Make sure that you do not have other problems.
- Have a plan for special events.
- Young people need to work at their problems as they have most to gain.

10

Putting it all Together

At the beginning of this book I said that there was a simple logic to agoraphobia, and that overcoming the problem was quite straightforward – and so it is. But I have never said that it was easy, and it isn't. The methods used to deal with agoraphobia are sensible and ordinary, but putting them into effect takes dedication and hard work, not just when you start to deal with your problem, but right through to the end. In fact it is fair to say that if agoraphobia is a problem for you, you will always have to be a little careful about the way you manage some public situations.

You need never worry that your agoraphobia will return. It will remain a ghost in your past, something which you have dealt with satisfactorily, and which you will always be able to deal with if it should ever rear its head again. The fact that you have overcome that particular problem will give you new confidence in yourself, and you shouldn't miss any opportunity which you are offered to capitalize on that new confidence. All this is something to work for – nothing more or less than the possibility of a new life, if that is what you seek. Why should it be so difficult to motivate yourself?

That is the problem of course – motivation. You have to do the exercises, to keep at it, keep practising and rehearsing, and that is a hard grind. It helps if you have someone to help you, either a professional or someone close to you, and that is something we will deal with later. Right now I would like to consider one other way in which you can help yourself.

Positive thinking

The last thing that someone who suffers from agoraphobia wants to hear is someone telling her to pull herself together. There may still be people in the world who have so little understanding that they take the attitude that all you have to do is get a grip on yourself and get on with it. You will know that you just can't do that, no matter how hard you try, and you probably have tried very hard in the past. You can't change your attitudes any more than you can change your physiology and make your adrenalin disappear. So what's all this about thinking positively?

I have left discussion of this matter until near the end of the book because I don't want anyone to think that I am suggesting that you can simply change your attitude at will, but there is a point to be made. People who suffer from agoraphobia tend to be diffident, and they suffer from a higher level of free-floating anxiety than others. That can mean that they tend to think negatively. They tend to see the glass of water as being half empty instead of half full, and are more likely than others to see good reasons why things cannot be done instead of reasons why they can.

These thought processes and attitudes are very subtle, and you may have a tendency to think negatively without being aware of it. If you could change that way of thinking it would surely help you to manage difficult situations and it would make the exercises and tasks in this book so much easier. It can work the other way around, of course. If you do the things suggested in this book you will begin to think more positively, so like everything else to do with agoraphobia it goes round in circles, but could you speed the defeat of your problem if you could develop the habit of thinking positively? The answer has to be yes. But how can you do it?

The positive diary

I'm almost afraid to mention diaries again as we have talked so much about them, but there is one last diary which you might want to keep and which could help you. The point of keeping a diary is to raise to a conscious level something which you currently take for granted, in this case your attitudes. What you should do now is to write down a few words not just about what you do, but also what you think about what you do. If you write an account of the past week, you may well find a lot of negative statements occurring – 'what if . . .', 'I can't . . . because I might . . .', 'I don't think I can . . .', and so on.

You might try writing a list of your own negative statements down one side of the paper, and opposite them a list of positive alternatives. You should get used to the language of the positive, because the next step is to rewrite your account of the week using only positive thoughts and ideas. Thinking negatively is a habit, and like all habits it can be relearned. You can get to a point when you suddenly notice that you have had a negative attitude and think, 'There I go again!'.

To help you along the way, make a note of your plans for the future, perhaps for the next week, but also for the longer term. Write it down as a little essay, but only allow yourself to use positive concepts. Say what you are going to do, not what you would like to do. If you are a woman planning a shopping trip you might write something like this:

> I will get up early and meet the girls at the station. We will get the eight-thirty train to the city and spend the first hour and a half in Centre Street. I want to go to Milton's but the others don't so I will go myself on a number 8 bus and I will meet them for lunch at Benny's. After lunch we will go to the cinema . . .

You can't change the way you think overnight, but if you talk in a positive way only, you will start to formulate positive ideas because that is all you have the language for, and positive ideas lead to positive acts and attitudes, and you may become more ambitious and more assertive. You have to learn the habit and simply not allow yourself to think in a negative way. Another advantage is that if you learn to talk in a positive way other people will become aware that you *sound* more assertive and they will treat you as if you are more assertive, and that will make it easier for you to act as if you are without having to make a conscious effort.

Sources of help

Agoraphobia is a condition which tends to isolate you. You may not be gregarious, but everyone needs the company of others, everyone needs help, and other people need your contribution. You cannot live in isolation and now that your agoraphobia is coming under control, you don't need to. If you are married or if you have a close relationship then it is easy for you to get the help which will shorten the recovery time from your agoraphobia. But if you have no one close who can you talk to?

Friends

If you have good friends you may find that they can be of great help to you. If the subject of your agoraphobia should arise in conversation – say, when you are explaining some difficulty you may have in going to an event of some sort – you may feel able to tell a friend. But be careful whom you take into your confidence. Not everyone understands agoraphobia, and people can be either very wary of psychological problems or else feel very threatened by them, probably because they feel vulnerable themselves. More usually, they just don't know how to respond, and if you unburden yourself to someone, no matter how close they may be, the result may not be what you expect.

If you do want to engage the help of a friend, ask them to do something specific. Ask them to go with you to a dance, or to stay with you if things aren't going well. Make sure that they know what is expected of them, otherwise they may not have the least idea how they can be of help, no matter how willing they may be.

Professional help

Most professional help is accessible through your doctor, and he or she is the best person to approach in the first instance. A sympathetic doctor may be able to offer adequate help and you may not need to go any further.

Doctors tend to favour treatment with medication, and there may sometimes be a place for the medical approach. If your main problem is related to your symptoms, then medication can relieve some of them. Things like diarrhoea or nausea can be treated, and there are drugs called beta blockers which are useful in 'performance anxiety', where a fast heart or palpitations can be a problem. They block some of the effects of adrenalin and performers like musicians, who need a steady hand, often find them helpful, and on occasion so might you.

The benzodiazepine group of drugs, once called tranquillizers, used to be commonly prescribed for people with psychological problems, but they are no longer used so much because of the risk of dependence. Many doctors don't prescribe them at all, but there is a place for their use in the short term, and there might be particular occasions where they might be of help.

Clearly the way forward does not lie entirely with drugs, and a good doctor will rely on a sympathetic ear and practical advice as the mainstay of his treatment. He may also be able to recommend other professionals who have special expertise in such problems as agoraphobia.

The person most likely to be of help to you is a clinical psychologist, someone who isn't a medical doctor but who has a university training in the way the mind works. They may use one of several different techniques, and a psychologist who favours the behavioural approach will use many of the ideas described in this book and will be able to help you with them and possibly take them further.

A psychologist may be able to organize group therapy, where people with similar problems can get together and discuss their difficulties without embarrassment. Such a group would hope eventually to do more than that, and a good group will develop an identity of its own and give support and motivation to its members, providing a strength which the individual members of the group couldn't achieve on their own. There are other techniques such as assertiveness training which might be of help if you feel that you aren't assertive enough, but for these techniques you need the co-operation of others and the help of professionals.

Help can also be obtained from charities and self-help groups which may be active locally. Your doctor may know of one, or there may be an advertisement in the local library or in the local press. Such organizations are run by individuals who understand your problem and can offer practical advice and help, or who may run groups which can give mutual support. Seek out the kind of help which suits you. If you are a private person then a 'one-to-one' approach may be best, but keep an open mind regarding the options. You may not like the idea of a group, but it could be that you need the support of a group if you are going to progress.

Other sources of help

The newspapers are full of advertisements for people who claim to be able to help with psychological problems such as agoraphobia. Some of them may be experienced and well qualified, and some may be self-taught and have little expertise. Such 'alternative' techniques as acupuncture, chiropractic, aromatherapy or hypnotherapy have their devotees and their place, but you have to be careful. It is my personal opinion that they have little value in the treatment of agoraphobia, and you should be wary of anyone who offers you an instant cure, because there is certainly no such thing. Overcoming agoraphobia will take hard work and much effort, and there are no short cuts. Think very hard and long before you part with your money.

The way forward

We are getting towards the end of this book. I hope that you can now see a way forward, a light at the end of a dark tunnel. I have been trying to impart a method of thinking about your problem, an approach to it which doesn't stop with the end of the book. You have to use your own imagination, your own invention and your determination to devise ways of continuing your assault on your agoraphobia. It is the approach which is as important as the actual exercises, the knowledge that there is a way forward which you can find if you keep an open mind and look for the right openings and paths.

If you suffer from agoraphobia you will know all about

loneliness, frustration and lack of fulfilment. Your agoraphobia may be very subtle, and you may not realize the extent to which it holds you back. You have to find out just how much it affects you and in what ways, and then you have to winkle it out. You can do that if you take it one step at a time. Getting rid of your agoraphobia is like climbing a long staircase out of a dark cellar. Don't miss any of the steps.

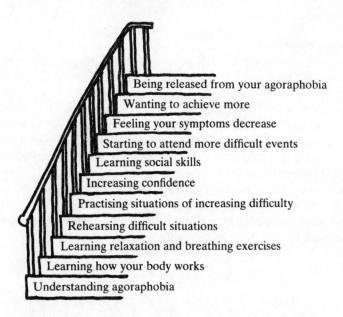

Being released from your agoraphobia
Wanting to achieve more
Feeling your symptoms decrease
Starting to attend more difficult events
Learning social skills
Increasing confidence
Practising situations of increasing difficulty
Rehearsing difficult situations
Learning relaxation and breathing exercises
Learning how your body works
Understanding agoraphobia

Gaining momentum

Nothing succeeds like success, and you don't have to take my word for it that any of the ideas and exercises in this book work. In fact you shouldn't take my word; you should prove it for yourself. The only way that you can improve your confidence is to have the courage actually to go to the places you want so much to go to and to find that you can not only survive in the difficult waters, but you can even enjoy the experience without anything untoward happening to you. None of the things that you fear may happen actually do happen, if you have done your homework and are properly prepared. Once you have proved that to yourself, and to your automatic nervous system, your fear of your symptoms will evaporate.

Once your fear of your symptoms has gone, your actual symptoms will also go and then you will be in the same boat as everyone else. You will still have difficult interviews or feel apprehensive before certain events, because that is normal for all of us and you are a normal person.

Once you have started to work on your problem, once you have had a few successes, your confidence will start to grow and your efforts to overcome your problem will gain momentum, like a snowball rolling down a snow-covered slope. It may start as a tiny snowball, but it gets bigger until it is an unstoppable avalanche. Your particular avalanche may be slow in getting started, and it may have a few bumps along the way, but in the end your efforts to overcome your agoraphobia will have their own momentum and, almost despite yourself, you will succeed.

If you haven't made a start, please do. If you have made a start, please continue even if you have setbacks, even if progress seems slow, even if the task should seem impossible. Remember, anything is possible, and many people just like you have overcome their agoraphobia and gone on to live rich, fulfilled lives. You can, too.

May I wish you the very best of luck.

Points to remember

- Learn to think positively.
- Be careful whom you get to help you.
- Professional help is available.
- Keep working at your problem.
- Agoraphobia can be overcome, and you can do it.

Index